How to Pass t

Safe Road User Award

Acknowledgements

Information in 'The driving test' section on pages 22–24 is adapted from material published on www.direct. gov.uk on the following web pages: www.direct.gov.uk/en/Motoring/LearnerAndNewDrivers/TheoryTest/ DG_4022534, www.direct.gov/uk/en/Motoring/LearnerAndNewDrivers/PracticalTest/DG_4022540 and www.direct.gov/uk/en/Motoring/LearnerAndNewDrivers/PracticalTest/DG_178328. This material is subject to Crown Copyright.

Answers to page 58 (on page 89) are adapted from www.safermotoring.co.uk and are reproduced with kind permission.

The Publishers would like to thank the following for permission to reproduce copyright material:
Photo credits p.1 and Unit 1 running head image © Ella Austin; p.6 (top) Map data © 2012 Google, (bottom) © jenny – Fotolia. com; p.12 © David Burton/Alamy; p.15 (top) © Bikeworldtravel – Fotolia.com, (bottom) © Ian Shaw/Alamy; p.16 (top) © Steven May/ Alamy, (bottom) © Driver and Vehicle Licensing Agency; p.17 © Ungor – Fotolia.com; p.18 © VOSA; p.19 © Studioshots/Alamy; p.28 © Crown Copyright; p.29 Map data © 2012 Google; p.32 © Will Stanton/Alamy; p.33 © Richard Peel/Alamy; p.48 (top to bottom) © Andrew Ward – Fotolia.com, © StudioPortoSabbia – Fotolia.com, (left) © Robert Wilson – Fotolia, (right) © Antrey – Fotolia.com, © Aleš Nowák – Fotolia.com; p.52 © StockImages/Alamy; p.53 © Becky Stares – Fotolia.com; p.55 (top) © Rob Wilkinson/Alamy, (bottom) © paul ridsdale/Alamy; p.61 and Unit 2 running head image © i love images/Alamy; p.65 © Tetra Images/Alamy; p.67 (top) © amidala – Fotolia.com, (bottom) © ANSA/PAT/ANSA/Corbis; p.74 © David J. Green – lifestyle themes/Alamy.
Every effort has been made to trace all copyright holders, but if any have been inadvertently overlooked the Publishers will be pleased to make the necessary arrangements at the first opportunity.

Although every effort has been made to ensure that website addresses are correct at time of going to press, Hodder Gibson cannot be held responsible for the content of any website mentioned in this book. It is sometimes possible to find a relocated web page by typing in the address of the home page for a website in the URL window of your browser.

Hachette Livre UK's policy is to use papers that are natural, renewable and recyclable products and made from wood grown in sustainable forests. The logging and manufacturing processes are expected to conform to the environmental regulations of the country of origin.

Orders: please contact Bookpoint Ltd, 130 Milton Park, Abingdon, Oxon OX14 4SB. Telephone: (44) 01235 827720. Fax: (44) 01235 400454. Lines are open 9.00–5.00, Monday to Saturday, with a 24-hour message answering service. Visit our website at www.hoddereducation.co.uk. Hodder Gibson can be contacted direct on: Tel: 0141 848 1609; Fax: 0141 889 6315; email: hoddergibson@hodder.co.uk

© Hodder & Stoughton Limited 2012
First published in 2012 by
Hodder Gibson
An Hachette UK Company
2a Christie Street
Paisley PA1 1NB

Impression number   5 4 3 2 1
Year   2014 2013 2012

Cover photos (left to right) © i love images / Alamy; © MBI / Alamy; © David Gee 1 / Alamy
Illustrations by Tony Wilkins and Cactus
Typeset in 9.5/12.5pt Frutiger by Phoenix Photosetting, Chatham, Kent
Printed in Dubai

A catalogue record for this title is available from the British Library

ISBN: 978 1444 122701

Contents

Introduction

This book is designed to accompany the SQA Safe Road User Award, whether you are studying this in school, at college or independently. Its main aims are to provide guidance and reminders about aspects of road safety, as well as practice tests and questions that will allow you to prepare for the assessments you will be required to sit as part of the Award. It is important to remember that the tests in this book are not the exact tests that you will sit under the Award. Some will follow a different format, but all will give you valuable practice and will allow you to test your knowledge in the run-up to your assessments.

For more detailed information on the exact nature of the Award assessments, the arrangements documents for this course can be viewed on the SQA website at **www.sqa.org.uk/sqa/35045.html**.

The following features are used to describe different activities within the book:

Think of a number
This activity is specifically designed to help you with your number skills.

Write it down
This activity is specifically designed to help you with your writing skills.

Web wonders
This activity requires you to use the Internet. The web page is always provided for you to use.

Think it through
This activity requires you to do an activity, an investigation or some research.

Did you know?
Some interesting facts about roads and road safety.

Attitudes
Some attitudes towards road safety that should be challenged or promoted.

The book consists of a number of chapters that relate directly to the two Units of the Safe Road User Award and the various tasks that are associated with each Unit:

Unit 1: Understanding how to use the roads

Task 1: Prepare for a journey by road

- Identify the modes of transport you could use for a journey
- Outline which is the most appropriate mode of transport in your circumstances
- Plan the best route for your journey
- Outline how you would decide if you and/or your companions are fit to travel

This task is assessed by the completion of a case study scenario.

Task 2: Identify what needs to be considered before going on a journey by road

- Outline the legal responsibilities of a road user
- State the documentation required for using a vehicle on the road
- Outline the safety checks that should be carried out before using a vehicle

This task is assessed by a short-response question test.

Task 3: Understand the road and use it safely

- Identify key elements of the **Highway Code**
- Identify road types, junctions and pedestrian crossings and describe their functions
- Identify traffic signals, road signs and markings
- Identify signals given by other road users
- Identify what to do at different junctions and crossings
- State the factors that affect a safe road speed
- Identify how different road users are affected by stopping distances
- Identify how and where to leave a vehicle safely and securely

This task is assessed by an online objective test. The questions in this test are based on the Highway Code.

Task 4: Describe how to use the roads with regards to the Highway Code and other road users

- Describe how to use the road in accordance with the principles of the Highway Code
- Outline why keeping up to date with changes in the Highway Code contributes to safe road use
- Describe the correct response to traffic signals, road markings, signals given by others and traffic control measures
- Describe what to do if you are in a vehicle that breaks down

- Describe what to do if you are involved in, or are a **witness** to, an incident

This task is assessed by a short-response question test.

Unit 2: Developing positive road user attitude

Task 1: Explain how attitudes of yourself and others can affect safe road use

- Identify own relevant characteristics
- Explain how these might impact on your road use
- Identify the relevant characteristics of others
- Explain how these might impact on their road use

This Unit is assessed by completing a personal learning agreement which is reviewed at various points throughout the course. This is designed to demonstrate your understanding of positive road user attitudes.

Task 2: Identify key factors to consider before setting out on a road journey

- Identify what makes an individual unfit to travel
- Identify the risks and responsibilities of carrying passengers, animals or goods
- Identify the legal requirements for travelling using a vehicle
- Identify why it is important to carry out regular vehicle safety maintenance

Task 3: Explain the importance of co-operating and communicating with other road users

- Explain how to communicate your intentions to other road users
- Consider the possible actions of other road users and explain how to respond and co-operate with them
- Explain how your behaviour might trigger negative behaviour in road users

On successful completion of the Safe Road User Award course, you will be eligible – within three years of the date on your certificate – to sit the abridged DSA driving theory test. This means that you have to pay less money and sit a shorter version of the test when you decide to get your licence. Good luck!

Statistics

Most of us will use the road every day, as **pedestrians**, drivers, **passengers** and cyclists, for example when we are going to school, to work, to the dentist, or to go shopping – the list is endless. With so many people using the roads it is important that we use them safely.

There were 230,905 road user **casualties** in 2008 – lower than in previous years.

- 2538 were killed – lower than in previous years.
- 26,034 were seriously injured – lower than in previous years.
- 202,333 were slightly injured – lower than in previous years.

The number of **fatalities** fell for most types of road users:

- Car occupants – 10% fall
- Pedestrians – 11% fall
- Motorcyclists – 16% fall
- Pedal cyclists – 15% fall.

The 2010 target of reducing the number of road deaths and serious injuries on roads by 40% was achieved. There are now plans for a more challenging target of reducing the number of deaths on the roads by one third by 2020.

If this target is going to be achieved, road users need to use the roads safely and demonstrate a positive and **responsible** attitude to safe road use.

Think of a number

In 2008 there were 230,905 road casualties.

By 2020 the aim is to reduce road casualties by a third.

What would be the number of road casualties in 2020 if we used the 2008 figure as a starting point?

The following example shows a similar calculation which might help you.

Example

2538 people were killed in road accidents in 2008.

If the target is to reduce this number by a third by 2020, then you would divide 2538 by 3.

2538 divided by 3 is 846. Subtract 846 from 2538.

This would leave the 2020 target as being no more than 1692 road deaths.

Did you know?

Icknield Way in Buckinghamshire is thought to be the oldest road in Britain.

Understanding how to use the roads

Prepare for a journey by road

Identify the modes of transport you could use for a journey

When considering **modes** of transport, we can think about how people or **goods** move from one place to another using air, roads, water or rail. In this book we are going to think mostly about modes of transport which use the road, but we will also look briefly at other modes that can be used as an alternative to the road, when appropriate.

Here are a few examples of the types of transportation that use the **road network**, including pavements:

- cars
- motorcycles
- buses
- lorries
- bicycles
- pedestrians.

Think it through

Think of some other modes of transport that might use the road network in the UK, other than the ones listed above.

Make a list of up to three modes of transport that could be used to carry people or goods by

- air
- rail
- sea.

Outline which is the most appropriate mode of transport in your circumstances

There are a number of factors that you might think about when deciding which mode of transport to take for a journey.

Distance

- Short distances might mean you can walk or cycle.
- Longer distances might mean you have to take the car, bus or train.
- For very long distances, for example travelling to Europe, you might think about the bus, train, ferry or aeroplane.

Skills

Are you qualified to drive a car? Can you ride a bicycle? The answers to these questions might **influence** your choice of mode of transport.

Cost

You need to consider the amount of money that you have available to fund the journey.

Number of people travelling

The number of people travelling on the journey will influence the choice of the mode of transport. A family of three might take the family car. A group of eight might take a minibus, bus or train.

Environmental factors

If you have a concern for the **environment**, you might consider modes of transport that have least impact on the environment, for example taking public transport such as the bus or train. Or you might use a car which has been designed to **minimise** impact on the environment.

Safety

Most journeys should be safe if properly planned. There are, however, **statistics** which show which modes of transport are the safest.

> **Did you know?**
>
> According to recent statistics, the chance of a person being killed when using a UK airline is 1 in 12.5 million. Compare this to the chance of being struck and killed by lightning, which is 1 in 10 million.

> **Think it through**
>
> Study the table below. Now answer the questions that follow, using the information provided.

Table 1.1 Risk of being killed by different modes of transport

Deaths per billion kilometres	Deaths per billion journeys	Deaths per billion hours
Air 0.05	Bus 4.3	Bus 11.1
Bus 0.4	Rail 20	Rail 30
Rail 0.6	Van 20	Air 30.8
Van 1.2	Car 40	Water 50
Water 2.6	Foot 40	Van 60
Car 3.1	Water 90	Car 130
Pedal cycle 44.6	Air 117	Foot 220
Foot 54.2	Pedal cycle 170	Pedal cycle 550
Motorcycle 108.9	Motorcycle 1,640	Motorcycle 4,840

Source: **http://www.numberwatch.co.uk/ risks_of_travel.htm**

1 Thinking about the distance travelled, which is the
   - safest mode of transport?
   - least safe mode of transport?

2 Which is the safest mode of transport when thinking about the total number of hours travelled?

3 Which mode of transport has a journey risk rating of 90?

4 Which mode of transport has a time rating of 220?

5 What conclusions can you make about motorcycling as a safe mode of transport?

6 What two modes of transport do you think are the safest?

Convenience

You need to consider the ease of getting to or using the mode of transport. It is easy to jump in your car, but perhaps not so easy to get to the nearest railway station, particularly if you have no other mode of transport.

Weather

This might be a consideration in relation to comfort. If it is raining or snowing or cold, then walking or using a motorcycle might not be ideal. Weather also needs to be considered when it comes to things like the expense of driving in snowy conditions, for example, or, more importantly, being able to stop safely for a hazard.

The weather might also be a factor if you don't have a lot of experience, or if you have just learnt to drive. Driving in the snow can be very challenging but it is a lot easier when you have got a bit more experience and practice under your belt.

> **Think it through**
>
> You are planning a short journey from Stirling (postcode FK10 3GJ) to Cumbernauld College (G67 1HU), a distance of some 20 miles. You have a choice of a motorcycle, a car or a bicycle. You will start the journey at noon in two days' time. There is no time pressure in terms of how long it takes you to get there. Look at the five-day weather forecast for this area using one of the following websites, and then select and justify a suitable mode of transport for this journey, given the weather forecast outlook.

Web wonders

http://www.metoffice.gov.uk/weather/uk/uk_forecast_weather.html

http://www.bbc.co.uk/weather/2643743

Write it down

Read the following case study and then write a short report detailing your preferred mode of transport, giving reasons for your choice. Your report should have the following headings:

- Journey title
- Starting point and time
- Finishing point and time
- Number of travelling passengers
- Preferred mode of travel
- Reasons for choice of mode of travel.

Attach any additional information to the end of your report.

Case study

You are travelling to the National Exhibition Centre in Birmingham from your school or college to attend a pop concert. You are travelling with three other friends, one of whom is eighteen and passed her driving test a month ago. The concert starts at 7p.m. and finishes at 10.30p.m.

Eco-driving

Increasing concern about the environment and the rising cost of petrol and diesel has led to an interest in ways of reducing fuel consumption for cars and other vehicles.

Eco-driving is a method of driving that allows the motorist to use fuel efficiently, and thus reduce the production of harmful **greenhouse gases**. It also turns out that if you drive in a way which reduces your fuel consumption you are also likely to be driving in a safe and responsible way.

Did you know?

The **AA** recently reported the results of an eco-driving test. Fifty-five AA members of staff undertook to drive normally for one week, and then drive using eco-driving methods in the second week. The staff reported an average saving of 10% on their fuel bills. One member of staff saved 33% on the cost of fuel.

We have already looked at some aspects of planning journeys and will look at more later in this Task (page 5). Later in the book we will also look at the importance of vehicle **maintenance** (page 69). These are both essential parts of eco-driving. However, when you are on your way, there are some simple steps to follow.

Leave promptly

When starting out on a journey, don't start the engine until you are ready to go – otherwise you are just wasting fuel.

In winter months use an ice-scraper to remove frost and ice rather than leaving the car running. This also reduces fuel waste.

Drive smoothly

A careful, smooth drive that minimises sharp braking and **erratic** acceleration will minimise fuel consumption. If you are stuck in a traffic jam or long queue for more than three minutes, the advice is that you should switch off your engine.

Decelerate smoothly

When slowing down or stopping, do so smoothly, as this will also reduce fuel consumption.

Change gear earlier

Gears should be changed at an engine speed of about 2000–2500 **r.p.m.**, depending on the fuel type.

Switch off the air conditioning

Some people think that, because a car is already travelling at 50 or 60 m.p.h., things like air conditioning come free. In fact, air conditioning can add as much as 10% to your fuel consumption. Remember that when it comes to energy nothing is free. In certain conditions, for example when driving in the city, it is equally effective simply to open your window.

Switch off unwanted devices

Turn off any devices that use up fuel, such as air blowers, radio and heated car seats, when they do not need to be used.

Follow speed limits

Speed limits are not only an important part of road safety strategy, they can help to minimise fuel consumption. Driving at 70 m.p.h. uses up approximately 9% more fuel than driving at 50 m.p.h.

Did you know?

Stagecoach is a worldwide bus operator which has recently announced plans to adopt an eco-driving system for all its bus services in the UK. From April 2011, 13,800 Stagecoach drivers will be following eco-driving methods in order to reduce greenhouse gas emissions, improve passenger comfort and reduce the potential for road accidents.

To help with eco-driving, car manufacturers are developing new eco-cars.

Think it through

Find out about each of the following types of eco-car:

- electric cars
- hybrid car
- cars using LPG.

Think of a number

A small bus company drives 2500 km a week, with fuel costs at £1.20 per litre. Each bus uses an average of 25 litres per 100 km.

How much money would the company save if it could reduce fuel consumption by 5% through eco-driving?

Attitudes

Many people have a poor attitude to eco-safe driving. If you ask them why they don't make the effort to drive in a way which saves fuel and is safer they will say things like:

'Other people don't drive that way, so why should I?'

'Even if I do drive eco-safely it will have no real effect globally.'

The important thing to remember here is that you are capable of making your own decisions. You do not have to do something just because other people do. Also, if you do try to practise eco-safe driving you are likely to save yourself money and to reduce the chances that you will be involved in a crash. Also, tests have shown that a person who is driving in an effective eco-safe way doesn't actually take much longer to reach their destination than somebody who is constantly accelerating and braking fiercely. Finally, if you start driving in an eco-safe way other people might have the confidence to drive that way and, if we all work together, we can make a difference on a global scale.

Plan the best route for your journey

Whatever journey you take, it is important to plan it in advance – to make sure that you get to your end destination safely and on time. Even a short journey to the shops by bus needs to be planned to make sure that you get to the bus stop at the correct time.

There are a number of different websites that are available to help you to plan journeys. Some specific examples include the following:

Web wonders

http://www.transportdirect.info/Web2/Home.aspx This allows you to plan a journey by train, flight, car, bus or even bicycle.

http://www.rac.co.uk/route-planner/ This allows you to plan a journey by road, using a car.

http://ojp.nationalrail.co.uk/en/s/planjourney/query This allows you to plan a journey by rail.

For other route planners, type 'route planner' into an Internet search engine.

Think it through

Use the transportdirect web link to complete the following activity.

Select the 'Day Trip Planner' on the left-hand menu.

You are going to plan a trip using the following information.

1   You will start the journey at the following postcode: EH22 1LE at 9.15a.m.

2   You will be travelling to visit the Falkirk Wheel, which is a visitor attraction in Falkirk. You will stay for two hours.

3   You will then travel back to Edinburgh to visit Edinburgh Castle, a Historic Scotland visitor attraction. You will stay there for two hours.

4   You will finish your journey at postcode EH22 1LE.

Print out your itinerary.

Of course there are other ways of trying to plan routes for journeys.

Using a road or street map

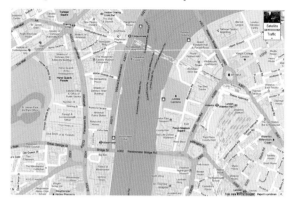

Map data © 2012 Google

This might be an option, particularly if it is a short journey or if you are walking.

Using a satnav

Satnav is a term used to describe a satellite navigation system which can be set up on a car and used to assist the driver with directions for a planned journey.

How does a satnav work?

Satnavs work by tapping into approximately twenty-four satellites that are located in space at different points in the world at any given time. These send a signal to the satnav which allows it to identify your exact position. This is done by means of the Global Positioning System (**GPS**). Typically a car satnav will tap into several satellites at any one time in order to identify your exact position and so calculate your planned route. This process continues until you have reached your final destination.

Web wonders

Watch the short videos on the following web links:

http://news.bbc.co.uk/1/hi/sci/tech/8643772.stm

http://www.youtube.com/watch?v=jzxm9pZPIok

Satnavs are commonly used by drivers to assist in journey planning. These have become more sophisticated over time and they can now be programmed to identify possible traffic jams and accidents and so help plan a different route. Using a satnav can not only reduce stress on long journeys, but can also lead to fuel economy and fewer stops to ask for directions, and less risk of having to turn back as a result of taking a wrong turning or exit.

However good satnavs might be, there are some sensible tips that need to be remembered to ensure safe driving:

1 Watch the road, not the satnav. Your focus must be on the road ahead and not on looking at the satnav screen. Satnav voice commands are a good idea, as long as they are not set so loud as to distract you.

2 What you see must take priority over what the satnav says. If it tells you to drive into a river, you should ignore the command. If the road looks wrong, don't take it.

3 Put the satnav in a sensible place; it should be seen easily, but it should not create a blind spot and block your view of the road.

4 Don't try to programme the satnav while driving, as this will distract you from the road ahead. Programme the satnav before you start your journey and pull over to adjust the setting if necessary.

5 Check the route is appropriate before you start. A satnav has different setting options, for example to avoid motorways. Check these before each journey.

6 Remember that thieves like satnavs too, so if it is detachable, always take it out when you leave the car. Thieves know that when people remove them they tend to keep them in the car, so mounts or suction cap marks might alert a thief to the fact that you have a satnav.

Did you know?

The first satnav designed for cars was developed in the 1980s.

Write it down

A product information sheet is a document that provides the consumer with some helpful information about a product. You can find an example at the web link below:

http://www.pixmania.co.uk/uk/uk/2126300/art/parrot/mki9000-bluetooth-in-car.html

Design a product sheet for a satnav of your choice. You will need to use the Internet to help you with this task. Your product sheet should include the following information:

- Summary of what the product does
- Main features of the product
- What the product comes with
- Manufacturer's name and model
- Product dimensions (sizes)
- Suggested price
- Illustration or image of the product
- Any accessories that might be available for the product
- Any other relevant information.

Your product information sheet should fit on one A4 sheet of paper.

Attitudes

It is important to remember the following points:

- Driving fast does NOT reduce time pressure.

7

- You should never attempt a risky driving manoeuvre (or one your driving instructor would not recommend), even if you consider yourself to be a skilled driver.

- Driving is NOT an innate skill, but is a learned one.

- Even if you use satnav, you should nevertheless plan a journey in advance – especially one you have not driven before.

- The desire to get somewhere quickly should NOT overrule the need to build in breaks for refreshment.

Outline how you would decide if you and/or your companions are fit to travel

There is a wide range of factors which can influence a person's fitness to travel, whether as a passenger **companion**, but particularly as a driver or rider, including on a bicycle or indeed on a horse. These influences include

- drugs
- alcohol
- tiredness
- emotional well-being
- physical health.

We will look at each of these in turn.

Drugs

By drugs we mean both legal drugs (drugs that you can obtain on prescription or legally buy from a supermarket or chemist) and illegal drugs.

One in five drivers or riders aged seventeen to eighteen admits to having driven under the influence of drink or drugs.

Drug driving is becoming as common a term as drink driving and is used to describe the situation when a person is taking a drug (legal or illegal) which might have a negative effect on driving. It is against the law to drive a vehicle while under the effects of an illegal drug and police officers now have powers to stop possible drug drivers and carry out roadside drug tests.

Legal drugs

Even drugs that you obtain with a doctor's prescription or buy legally from the supermarket or chemist can influence your ability to travel. Some may make your feel drowsy or tired and so you should always read the instructions or warning on all medicine that you take in advance of travel.

Antihistamines are legal drugs that are sometimes used to treat hay fever. However, they can have side effects that can affect your ability to drive.

It can be particularly dangerous if you have to take two or three different drugs at the same time. While each one may be perfectly safe, the combination may create negative side-effects.

Web wonders

Type 'side effects of antihistamines' into an Internet search engine such as Google.

What might be the side effects of taking these drugs and how might they affect your ability to drive?

Illegal drugs

There are drugs that are classified as being illegal for people to buy, usually because they have some dangerous side effects. Different drugs have different effects on your ability to drive. Let's look at one common illegal drug: cannabis.

Cannabis is an illegal drug that is usually smoked. It has a negative effect on driving because it reduces your ability to concentrate. Cannabis can also make you feel tired, make you lose your sense of direction and make you feel **anxious** about your surroundings – all of which would have a negative effect on your driving ability. It is thought that smoking cannabis has a similar effect on driving as drinking four pints of beer. It leaves a trace in your body which can be detected by tests for up to four weeks after use.

Did you know?

Recent research has indicated that as many as 800,000 UK drivers a year might be operating vehicles under the influence of cannabis. In a recent study, drivers not under the influence of cannabis had an average stopping distance of 270 feet when driving at 66 m.p.h. This increased to 310 feet after smoking cannabis.

Think it through

Investigate the effects of two of the following illegal drugs on a person's ability to drive.

- Cocaine
- LSD
- Heroin
- Ecstasy
- Speed

Penalties

The **penalty** for drug driving is the same as the penalty for drink driving – a ban and a fine of up to £5000 or six months in prison. This increases to a two-year ban and a maximum of ten years in prison if a person drug driving causes a fatal accident.

Unlike driving under the influence of drink, there are no set legal limits on how much substance you should have in your body, nor is there a specific test that can be given to assess how much of an illegal substance you have in your body. However, the police can stop you if they suspect you are driving under the influence of drugs.

If a person is stopped under the suspicion of driving under the influence of drugs, police can carry out simple tests that might provide an indication of drug use. You could be asked to perform a co-ordination test such as being asked to close your eyes and touch your nose, or to stand on one leg for a short period of time. If you refuse to do such tests, as with failing to provide a breath test if suspected of drink driving, this is an **offence**.

Alcohol

It is against the law to drive any vehicle (including a bicycle) on a road when under the influence of drink. If convicted you could face a fine, a driving ban, **community service** or possibly a prison sentence.

The UK legal drink driving limit is usually given in terms of **BAC**, blood–alcohol concentration.

The maximum legal BAC in the UK is:

35 microgrammes of alcohol per 100 millilitres of breath

OR

80 milligrammes of alcohol per 100 millilitres of blood

OR

107 microgrammes of alcohol per 100 millilitres of urine.

Alcohol affects a driver's judgement, co-ordination and **reactions**, particularly with regard to stopping distances. This makes the driver a risk to passengers and other road users.

Did you know?

- Approximately 3000 people are seriously injured or killed each year in the UK as a result of driving under the influence of drink.
- One in six deaths on UK roads involve people who are under the influence of drink and over the legal alcohol limit.
- Males aged between 17 and 29 are most likely to be involved in drink driving incidents.
- If you drink alcohol at a party in the evening you could still be above the legal limit at lunch time the following day.
- Alcohol is excreted from your body at a rate which is controlled by your liver. There are no ways to artificially speed up this process. Drinking coffee, for example, doesn't have any effect and won't sober you up.

Penalties

Drink driving is punished by **disqualification** and **penalty points** and can also lead to a fine or a jail sentence. The table below shows the maximum penalties for drink driving.

Table 1.2 **Maximum penalties for drink driving**

Offence	Jail sentence	Fine	Disqualification	Penalty points
Causing death by careless driving under the influence of drink/drugs	14 years	Unlimited	**Obligatory** 2 years minimum	3–11
Driving while unfit through drink/drugs	6 months	£5000	Obligatory	3–11

Source: **http://www.drivingban.co.uk/drivingoffencespenalties.htm**

Web wonders

Use the Internet to find out more about each of the following terms:

- The 'totting up' system
- TT99
- New Drivers Act

Did you know?

It is very common for people who are tired to fall asleep for a few seconds or minutes without even realising that they have done so. This is particularly likely to happen on motorways, which can be monotonous, or at night. If you nodded off for 6 seconds while driving at 70 m.p.h. on a motorway, you would have travelled nearly 200 metres while you were asleep.

Tiredness/fatigue

Driver or rider tiredness or **fatigue** accounts for about one in five accidents on major roads, which means about 300 road deaths per year.

Tiredness affects your performance and alertness. It increases the amount of time you need to react to a situation. It can cause memory problems and reduced co-ordination. Tiredness can badly affect your ability to drive safely and so causes a danger to other road users.

There are a number of tips that you can follow to help minimise the effects of tiredness.

- Take plenty of rest before you start a long drive. If you feel tired, do not drive.
- Take a break every one to two hours, depending on the driving conditions.
- If you start to feel tired, stop and have a 20-minute break to take a quick nap, get some fresh air and have a cup of coffee or energy drink.

Web wonders

Watch the following video clip:

http://www.youtube.com/ watch?v=unfKWtQkqUo

List the signs of tiredness that you observed in the video clip.

Emotional well-being

Emotional well-being is how you feel about yourself and other people. Our emotions can have an impact on our ability to drive safely and so impact on other road users. Here is an example:

Write it down

Jayne has been to visit her mum in hospital and has just found out that she is seriously ill. Jayne drives home, but she is very upset and starts to cry. For a moment she is not concentrating on the road and hits the kerb.

In this situation Jayne's emotions have affected her ability to drive safely and this might endanger other road users.

Write one sentence to explain each of the following emotions and then explain how each emotion might affect your ability to drive safely:

- happiness
- fear
- anger
- aggressiveness.

Did you know?

Before you start to learn to drive, you need to make sure that your eyesight meets the minimum requirements. At the start of any practical driving test the examiner will ask you to read the number plate on a parked vehicle at these distances:

- 20 metres for vehicles with new-style number plates
- 20.5 metres for vehicles with old-style number plates.

If you normally wear glasses or contact lenses in order to meet this requirement, you should wear these when driving.

Physical health

When driving a vehicle on a public road, you have responsibility for the safety not only of yourself, but also of passengers and other road users. It is important that you are aware of any health issue that might affect your ability to use the road safely. In addition, if you are aware of any health condition that might affect your ability to drive, you should see your doctor immediately. The following health conditions in particular can affect your ability to drive safely.

Poor eyesight

Your eyesight is vital to safety when driving on any road. Good eyesight is essential if you are to see far enough ahead to identify oncoming traffic and observe possible **hazards**, and to spot the people or vehicles moving in your **peripheral** vision. You also need to be able to identify the different colours of traffic lights. It is important that you have your eyes tested regularly to make sure that your vision meets minimum requirements, as this is a legal requirement and a responsibility of all drivers.

Heart problems and serious health problems

If a serious condition such as a heart problem is identified, you should consult your doctor in order to ensure that you are still fit enough to operate a vehicle. If you fail to do this, there might be a risk that you could cause an accident.

Diabetes and epilepsy

Web wonders

Use the Internet to find out about diabetes and epilepsy and write a short sentence to explain why it might be dangerous to drive with these conditions.

When you have been diagnosed with any condition that is likely to affect your ability to drive you must inform the **DVLA**. You may be asked to hand back your driving licence. It is a criminal offence to continue to operate a vehicle when you have certain serious health conditions.

You must not operate a vehicle if you suffer from an alcohol or drug addiction.

Attitudes

It is important to remember the following points:

- Driving and riding need your FULL attention.
- Fatigue IS a contributor to serious crashes.
- Having a cup of coffee, winding down the window or listening to music will NOT reduce fatigue.
- Fatigue does NOT only occur on long journeys, or mainly on country roads.
- There ARE consequences for driving or riding while fatigued (the police can detect a fatigued driver).
- The assumption that most fatigue-related crashes occur at night is WRONG.
- Driving or riding while fatigued is JUST as dangerous as driving while drunk or speeding.
- Driving or riding close to others will NOT encourage them to drive faster, but will endanger yourself and others.

Age and safe road use

Getting older does not mean that you inevitably become a worse driver or rider. As you get older you learn to understand what is happening on the road around you and to recognise and understand what is happening in your body. This means that many older drivers are very skilled and very competent. However, it is also the case that elderly people may have an increased feeling of anxiety or nervousness in certain driving situations, for example, while driving at night, because of problems with eyesight. Or they might worry that they are driving more slowly than other motorists, so causing them frustration.

As we become older, our bodies start to change. Our muscles can weaken, we become less flexible and

our joints may start to stiffen – we just don't feel as fit as we used to. This can make certain aspects of driving more difficult, such as being able to carry out an emergency stop, manoeuvring the steering wheel, or carrying out essential observation checks before signalling.

In addition, hearing and vision, particularly night vision, tend to decline. Impaired hearing may make it difficult to hear an approaching emergency vehicle or train.

Here are some simple common-sense tips for elderly drivers, most of which are a good idea for younger drivers too!

- Hearing and eyesight tests should be taken regularly.
- If you are taking **medication**, ask your doctor if it might have any impact on your ability to drive: for example, will it cause **drowsiness**?
- Keep fit, as this can help with mobility and with some driving manoeuvres, such as turning the steering wheel.
- Drive at times when the road conditions will be less stressful: for example, driving during the rush hour can be stressful.
- Plan your journey in advance to minimise stress and anxiety.
- Don't drink and drive.

End of Task test

Answer each of the following questions by selecting the correct answer: A, B, C or D.

1 Which of the following modes of transport is not motorised?

A Scooter

B Bicycle

C Car

D Motorcycle

2 Which of the following modes of transport might be best to use when it is raining heavily?

A Car

B Motorcycle

C Bicycle

D Scooter

3 Which mode of transport is considered the most dangerous in terms of fatalities?

A Aeroplane

B Car

C Motorcycle

D Van

4 What does GPS stand for?

A Global Positioning System

B Global Positioning Satellite

C Grand Prix Stadium

D General Positioning System

5 What is the main purpose of a satnav?

A To tell you how much fuel your vehicle is using

B To tell you how much CO_2 your vehicle is emitting

C To tell you the best route to take for a journey

D To tell you the position of the nearest motorway

6 What is the possible penalty for drug driving?

A Disqualification and a fine of £5000 or six months in jail

B Community service

C Disqualification and ten years in prison

D A fine of £1000 and 3 penalty points on your licence

7 What is the legal drink driving limit in the UK?

A 15 microgrammes of alcohol per 100 millilitres of breath

B 35 microgrammes of alcohol per 100 millilitres of breath

C 80 microgrammes of alcohol per 100 millilitres of breath

D 107 microgrammes of alcohol per 100 millilitres of breath

8 Which of the following will help to prevent tiredness when driving?

A Sing to yourself

B Open the window for air

C Take a 20-minute break and have a quick nap

D Turn up the radio

9 Which of the following emotions might appear in someone who has road rage?

A Happiness

B Aggression

C Patience

D Sadness

10 Which of the following conditions might mean that you have to surrender your driving licence?

A Epilepsy

B Flu

C Headache

D Food poisoning

Task 2

Unit 1 Understanding how to use the roads

Identify what needs to be considered before going on a journey by road

Once you have planned your journey – whether as a person in charge of a vehicle or as a passenger, cyclist or pedestrian – there are a number of other factors that need to be considered.

Outline the legal responsibilities of a road user

As a road user, your main responsibility is to understand and observe the Highway Code. This is dealt with in other sections of the book. However, the Highway Code is intended for all road users, not just the drivers of vehicles.

Pedestrians

Pedestrians are one of the most **vulnerable** groups of road users in the UK. The Highway Code provides a range of rules that should be followed by pedestrians.

- Pedestrians should always use the pavement when one is provided. If there is no pavement, walk on the side of the road facing the traffic coming towards you.
- Pedestrians should use pedestrian crossings to cross roads when they are provided: for example, zebra crossings, pelican crossings or other means such as footbridges and underpasses.
- Always stop, look and listen before crossing a road and never cross a road in between parked vehicles, as they can block your vision.
- Children should use school crossing patrols if they are available.
- When crossing the road you should walk rather than run, in case you trip and fall.
- Never fool about beside a road; playing football or other games on the road is very dangerous.

Did you know?

- Over 4200 pedestrians are involved in accidents in the UK each year, the majority of which happen in built-up areas such as those near schools.
- Pedestrians account for a quarter of all road deaths.
- The 5–14 age group is most at risk from pedestrian accidents, probably because they have less experience of road use. Almost a third of all pedestrian accidents occur on the way to or from school.

It is for these reasons that there have been schemes set up to try to establish safe walking and cycling routes to schools.

Think it through

Identify a secondary and a linked primary school in your neighbourhood. Using a street map or other resources, develop a safe walking route that could be followed by the primary school children who have to walk to the secondary school in order to take part in an out-of-school activity.

Your safe walking route should include the following:

- map showing the proposed walking route
- area that might be particularly dangerous, explaining why, and suggesting what could be done to reduce the danger.

14

Cyclists

There are specific legal requirements for people using bicycles on the road.

- It is against the law to cycle on the pavement or a footpath unless it is specifically marked to show that cyclists can use it.

- Cyclists are not allowed to carry passengers unless the cycle has been specifically designed for the purpose.

- Bikes ridden at night need to have front and rear lights.

- Bikes should be fitted with a red rear reflector and newer bikes should have amber pedal reflectors fitted.

- All Highway Code rules and **regulations** apply to cyclists, for example not using a mobile phone when cycling, observing traffic signs, and so on.

- Although there is no **legislation** in place, the Highway Code says that cyclists should wear a cycle helmet that conforms to current regulations.

- There is no requirement to pass a **cycling proficiency test**, but if you have the chance to take one, it will help you stay safe on the roads.

Think it through

Wearing a cycle helmet does seem like a common-sense approach to road safety.

Design a poster that could be displayed in a local primary school which provides some common-sense rules for using a cycle safely.

Web wonders

For an example of a safe cycling poster visit the following website:

http://www.playgroundbasics.co.uk/catalogue/safety/safe-cycling-sign/safe-cycling-sign-2

Cycle routes or cycle tracks are special paths designed for use by cyclists. In some towns and cities, special lanes in roads have been set aside for cyclists to ensure that they have a safer road journey.

Web wonders

Visit the following website and find the nearest cycle route to where you live.

http://www.cycle-route.com

Make a printout of the cycle route.

Motorcyclists

There are specific legal requirements for people using motorcycles on the road.

As well as requiring the correct vehicle documentation, you must wear an approved safety helmet. All helmets in the UK must comply with specific safety requirements.

A helmet is not only a legal requirement for riding a motorcycle, it is also an essential item of protection because it protects the head from injury in the event of an accident, as well as protecting the face and eyes from flying objects such as flies and **debris** from the road. A helmet can also protect your head from cold and wind. A full-face helmet is recommended.

You should never wear a helmet which has been involved in a crash or has been dropped on a hard surface. This type of contact can create micro-fractures in the helmet's structure which can seriously damage the helmet and mean that it will not give you the amount of protection that it should.

Motorcyclists can carry a **pillion passenger** *if they hold a full driving licence.* There is no specific requirement for protective or safety clothing, but it is sensible for both motorcyclist and passenger to wear appropriate protective clothing – such as bike leathers – and **fluorescent** clothing or accessories if the light is poor. Remember that even if it is fairly warm when you are walking around it will feel much colder when you are riding. If you let your hands or feet get cold you may not be able to operate the controls as quickly or effectively.

State the documentation required for using a vehicle on the road

In order to drive and own a vehicle on the road there are specific legal requirements that must be followed.

The following items of documentation are mandatory if you own and use a vehicle on the road:

- Driving licence
- **MOT** certificate (if applicable)

- Vehicle excise licence
- Vehicle registration certificate
- Motor insurance.

Driving licence

A driving licence is mandatory.

It is issued by the DVLA.

Driver and Vehicle
Licensing Agency

Think it through

Find out more information about the DVLA and what they do.

Provisional licence

At the age of seventeen you can apply to obtain your **provisional licence**. You need to have your provisional driving licence before you can start driving lessons or sit your driving theory or practical tests. You have to complete the correct form in order to apply for your driving licence. This can be obtained from

- the post office
- the DVLA office
- the DVLA website (**www.dvla.gov.uk**).

The D1 form has to be completed fully, with two passport-sized photos included. These help with ensuring that you are who you say you are when driving a car or sitting your driving test. One picture will appear on your driving licence and the other is kept by DVLA. You also need to include the relevant application fee.

> **Think it through**
>
> Find out the current fee for a provisional driving licence.
>
> Download and complete a copy of a D1 form.

The photographs, just as when you apply for a passport, need to be authenticated by a professional person, such as a doctor or school teacher. This is to reduce the possibility of a person applying for a driving licence in another person's name. When you have your driving licence you should carry it with you, especially when you are taking driving lessons.

If you are sixteen years old you can apply for a **moped** licence. When you have obtained it, you are permitted to ride a moped and carry a pillion passenger.

Learning to drive with a provisional licence

Whatever vehicle you plan to drive, it is important that you let other road users know if you are a learner driver. This means that the vehicle that you drive must have L-plates fitted to the front and rear of the vehicle. This includes scooters and motorcycles. It is an offence not to display L-plates.

As a learner drive, you must be accompanied by another driver (unless on a scooter or motorcycle) and this person must be at least 21 years old and have held a full driving licence for at least three years.

Learner drivers are not allowed to drive on a motorway.

Full driving licence

When you have successfully completed your driving test, you can apply to change your provisional licence to a full licence, which will allow you to drive the same category of vehicle in which you passed your driving test. You will need to send your provisional licence with form D1. You will also need to send the appropriate fee and passport-sized photographs. Your new licence will indicate the types of vehicles that you are able to drive, which for most people would include

- car
- motorcycle
- **LGV** or **PCV** vehicle
- minibus.

However, you will need to pass additional tests to show competence to drive these other vehicles.

You new licence will be in the form of a photocard, along with a paper licence. The photocard was introduced to reduce driving fraud (for example, driving with a licence that belongs to another person) and holds all your details electronically as well as displaying your photograph. Since the introduction of the photocard licence, drivers are required to renew their licence every ten years. Failure to do so is an offence. It is also important to inform DVLA if you change your address.

Remember, after you have passed your test, you can start to drive as a full licence holder, even though you still have to receive your full UK driving licence. Your driving test examiner may ask you if you wish him/her to retain your provisional driving licence to submit to DVLA for converting to a full licence. This might be helpful, but if you need your provisional driving licence as proof of age for other purposes, it might be more convenient to return your licence yourself at another time.

MOT certificate

MOT stands for Ministry of Transport. MOT certification is a mandatory test for all vehicles over the age of three years to ensure that the vehicle is roadworthy and meets current environmental standards.

The test is referred to as an MOT, and lasts for one year, although it can be renewed at any time within the last month of validity. If your MOT runs from 1 January to 31 December, you can renew your MOT at any time from 1 December to 31 December.

It is against the law to drive without a valid MOT if your vehicle is over three years old. In addition you will not be able to apply for a tax disc unless you hold a valid MOT document. It is worth remembering that if you drive without an MOT you risk a fine and, if you are involved in an accident, your insurance will be invalid.

It is straightforward to obtain an MOT for your vehicle, so there is no excuse for not having one. There are hundreds of garages which can carry out an MOT test on your car. These garages are registered with the Vehicle Operator and Services Agency (**VOSA**) and are equipped and have mechanics trained to carry out MOTs. To minimise fraud, all MOTs are now recorded electronically in a database held by VOSA.

The location of all VOSA-registered MOT stations can be found in the Yellow Pages or online.

The MOT is designed to test various aspects of your vehicle to make sure it is roadworthy and meets current environmental standards. These tests are specified in law. Specifically an MOT covers the following areas:

- lights (including indicators, headlights, brake lights)
- seatbelts
- areas of rust
- brakes
- steering
- gears
- emissions.

So what happens if your vehicle fails the MOT? You can have another MOT undertaken, after you have sorted out the faults that were identified. Of course, you have to pay for another MOT! This means that although your car has failed the MOT, you would be able to drive it to another garage for the necessary repairs. This is the only occasion on which you can drive a car without a valid MOT; however, you should check this with your insurance company before starting such a trip.

> **Think it through**
>
> Find the details of your nearest MOT centre and the current cost of an MOT for a car and a motorcycle.

Vehicle excise duty

Vehicle Excise Duty (**VED**), sometimes referred to as car or vehicle tax, is a tax that each vehicle owner has to pay in order to use public roads. VED is collected by the DVLA. Vehicle tax is required for most vehicles using the roads. When you have paid your vehicle tax, you will be issued with a tax disc which must be displayed on the vehicle. You can apply for a new tax disc via post, online or even by text. When you apply for a vehicle tax disc, DVLA will check their database to make sure that you have an MOT and valid insurance for the vehicle concerned.

If you plan to keep your vehicle off the road for a period of time and do not wish to pay road tax, you should complete a Statutory Off Road Notification (**SORN**).

Think it through

Find out the current VED rates for the
following classification of vehicles:

- band A car
- band H car
- band M car
- motorcycle over 600 cc.

Vehicle Registration Certificate

The Vehicle Registration Certificate (V5C), commonly
known as the 'logbook', is a certificate that is issued
when a vehicle is registered with the DVLA. The V5C
is sent to the registered keeper, who is the person
responsible for registering and taxing the vehicle.
This might not be the owner of the vehicle.

A vehicle registration document contains various
information including

- vehicle keeper's name and address
- vehicle registration number
- other relevant information about the vehicle such
  as the make, vehicle identification number (VIN)
  and number of previous keepers (if not a brand
  new car).

You should always obtain a Vehicle Registration
Certificate when you purchase a car, whether new or
secondhand.

Motor insurance

It is against the law to drive a vehicle on a public road
if you do not have motor insurance. There are
different types of motor insurance available:

- third party insurance
- third party, fire and theft insurance
- comprehensive insurance.

Third party insurance

Third party insurance is the most basic type of vehicle
insurance that you can purchase and it is usually the
cheapest, because it provides the lowest type of
protection for you and your vehicle.

It covers you only in the case of an accident and even
then it only covers the cost relating to the other
party. This means that if you crashed into another
vehicle, and it was your fault, neither you nor your
vehicle would be covered, only that of the other
person involved in the accident. This would cover
injury to the other person, their property and their
vehicle. This means that you would have to pay for
the cost of getting your own vehicle towed away and
repaired if necessary.

Third party, fire and theft insurance

Third party, fire and theft insurance offers an
increased level of protection. As well as offering the
protection of third party, it protects your vehicle
against theft and fire. Even for third party, fire and
theft it is important to remember that in the event of
an accident it only covers the cost relating to the
other party. Third party, fire and theft insurance will
be more expensive than third party.

Comprehensive insurance

Fully comprehensive insurance is the most expensive
type of insurance, because it covers you against most
eventualities. As well as offering the protection of
third party, fire and theft, it also covers you and your
vehicle. Generally it covers the following:

- theft
- accidental damage
- criminal damage

- injury to others
- injury to yourself
- damage to personal belongings
- fire damage
- medical expenses.

Comprehensive insurance usually comes with a range of extras including the following:

- Legal fees: if you are sued by the other party, your legal fees will be paid.
- Courtesy vehicle: if your vehicle needs to be repaired, the insurance company will organise for you to have a replacement vehicle for the period of time in which you car is off the road.
- Breakdown cover: if your car breaks down, or is involved in an accident, a breakdown company (such as the AA or **RAC**) would either try to repair your vehicle or take you to the nearest garage where you can get further assistance. They may also offer to take you home or to your planned destination (if not your home).
- Windscreen cover: if your vehicle has its windscreen chipped, cracked or broken, you will be entitled to a repair or replacement. This is normally undertaken at a time and place convenient to you.
- No claims bonus: if you do not make a **claim** against your insurance within a one-year period, you may be entitled to a discount on your insurance cost for the following year – because you are regarded as a lower-risk driver! You can even protect your no claims bonus; this means that even if you do have an accident you would still be considered for a discount on the **premium**.

Of course, all these extra benefits add to the cost of your insurance so you need to think carefully about each of these before you sign up for any insurance policy.

The cost of motor insurance

Motor insurance can be expensive, particularly for new, inexperienced and young drivers. There are a number of factors that affect your motor insurance cost:

- make, performance, engine capacity, vehicle security and the age of the vehicle
- age and/or experience of the driver, driving record, area of residence and type of use
- type of cover.

Did you know?

Insurance for young drivers is so expensive, not because of the costs of the cars but because of the costs that arise from young people who are severely injured and require care for the rest of their lives.

Think it through

Complete the table below by ticking the appropriate column to show which factors you think would increase or decrease insurance costs.

Table 1.3 Factors affecting the cost of insurance

Description of factor	Increase insurance cost	Decrease insurance cost
An experienced driver of 15 years with no accidents and no penalty points on his licence		
A new male driver aged 19		
A new male driver aged 35		
A car with built-in car alarm and engine immobiliser		
Driver of a Porsche car		
Owner of a 5-year-old 1-litre Fiat Punto		
Car which is parked in a secure garage overnight		
Third party only insurance cover		
Car which is parked on the street in the city centre at night		

Think it through

Find out what each of the following insurance terms means:

- policy excess
- cover note
- renewal notice
- policy document
- premium.

There is likely to be a time in every driver's life when they have to contact the insurance company to make a claim for damage to their vehicle, or damage to another person's vehicle. If you are involved in an accident, you must report this to your insurance company as soon as possible and provide them with the following information:

- policy details including your name and address.

They will ask about the circumstances of your claim and may ask for other information, such as:

- the names and addresses of others involved in the incident
- the nature of the damage to vehicle
- the Crime Number (if the police have been involved).

Reporting an accident can be stressful, but it is important to keep calm. The insurance company will send you documents to be completed so that they can process your insurance claim. If you were involved in an accident, these documents may ask for some very specific information, such as:

- a statement from the police
- any **eye-witness** statements
- the police incident report
- any photographic evidence
- **quotations** for repairs
- a copy of your driving licence.

It is therefore important that when you are involved in an accident you try to gather as much of this information as possible. It is a good idea to sit down

and write up some notes about the accident as soon as you can after it happens. You will find that you forget details very quickly if you don't. A good way to do this is to use a formula, such as: Day, Date, Time, Place, I saw... So, for example:

'On Monday the 13th February 2012, at 0930, on the dual carriageway section of the A52, half way between the Ratcliffe RSPCA junction and the Gamston roundabout, I saw a blue Mercedes Benz, registration number AB12 ABC driving towards Nottingham at a high speed...'

Other aspects of legislation

New Drivers Act (1995)

In 1995, the Government introduced a piece of legislation called the New Drivers Act. The Act was introduced to try to promote safer driving among those who have just passed their test. Normally a driver can lose their licence if they collect more than 12 penalty points, for example, for offences such as speeding. Under the New Drivers Act this limit is reduced to 6 points within the first two years after passing their test. This means that it only takes a couple of convictions to have your licence taken away. The Act also says that, if you do lose your licence in this way, you will have to take your test again to get it back.

Mobile phone legislation

Many people own a mobile phone, but it is now illegal to use a mobile when driving a vehicle. You can be stopped by the police and charged. The penalty is three penalty points and a fine, which can range between £60 and £2500. You can use a hands-free set, but again you need to ensure that the operation of the phone and the conversation that you are having does not distract you from driving. You should not text while driving, as this is probably even more dangerous than having a phone conversation.

Compulsory Basic Training (CBT)

As a learner rider of a scooter or motorcycle, you need to have completed CBT in order to ride on the road. There are some exceptions to this rule:

- if you passed a full moped test after December 1990

- if you have a Certificate of Completion
- if you have a full driving licence (issued before February 2001) for a car and intend to ride a moped.

When you have completed CBT you will be given a certificate called DL196. You must produce this before you can take the practical motorcycle test.

Attitudes

It is important to remember the following points.

- It is NEVER acceptable to drive or ride without car insurance.
- It is NEVER acceptable to drive or ride without a valid MOT.
- It is NEVER acceptable to drive without a valid driving licence.
- It is NOT fine to drive an unroadworthy car for short distances/on minor roads/if driving it to the garage to be fixed.
- Gaining a driving licence is NOT a right, but is a privilege.
- If you ever wonder 'Other people drive unroadworthy cars, so why can't I?', remember that driving a car that is not roadworthy endangers yourself as the driver, your passengers and other road users around you.

The driving test

Before you can move from a provisional to a full driving licence, you need to pass your driving test. This comes in two parts: a test of theory and a practical driving test.

Cars: Theory test

The theory test is made up of a multiple choice part and a hazard perception part. You need to pass both parts to pass the theory test. Once you've passed it you can apply to take your practical driving test.

Multiple choice section

Before the test starts you'll be given instructions on how it works. You can choose to do a practice

session of multiple choice questions to get used to the layout of the test. At the end of the practice session the real test will begin. A question and several possible answers will appear on a computer screen – you have to select the correct answer. Some questions may need more than one answer. You can move between questions and 'flag' questions that you want to come back to later in the test. Some car and motorcycle questions will be given as a case study. The case study will

- present you with a short story about a driving situation and ask you to answer five questions based on the information in that story
- focus on real-life examples and experiences that you could come across when driving.

The test will last for a maximum of 57 minutes and you need 43 marks out of 50 to pass.

Hazard perception section

Before you start the hazard perception part, you'll be shown a short video clip about how it works. You'll then be shown a series of video clips on a computer screen. The clips

- feature everyday road scenes
- contain at least one developing hazard (but one of the clips will feature two developing hazards).

A developing hazard is something that may result in you having to take some action, such as changing speed or direction. The earlier you notice a developing hazard and make a response, the higher you will score. The most you can score for each developing hazard is five points.

To get a high score you need to

- respond to the developing hazard during the early part of its development
- press the mouse button as soon as you see a hazard developing.

You will be shown fourteen clips, with fifteen developing hazards and you need to score 44 marks out of 75 in this section.

At the end of the test you will be given your result by the test centre staff.

Practical test

The driving test for a car is designed for you to show that you can drive safely and responsibly on the road and that you can apply your knowledge of the Highway Code and theory correctly. Throughout the test your examiner will be looking for an overall safe standard of driving, including when you are carrying out the set exercises.

After meeting your examiner, two stages will follow:

- An eyesight check – if you fail this, your test will not continue.
- Your examiner will ask you two questions about carrying out vehicle safety checks.

You'll be asked one 'show me' and one 'tell me' question. One or both questions answered incorrectly will result in one driving fault being recorded.

The driving part of your test will last about 40 minutes, during which you will be examined on your general driving and ability to reverse your vehicle safely. One exercise will be chosen from

- reversing around a corner
- turning in the road
- reverse parking.

You may also be asked to carry out an emergency stop exercise.

Throughout the test you should drive in the way your instructor has taught you. If you make a mistake, don't worry about it as it might be a less serious driving fault and may not affect your result. However, if at any time your examiner considers your driving to be a danger to other road users your test will be stopped.

Your practical driving test will include approximately ten minutes of independent driving. This is designed to assess your ability to drive safely while making decisions independently.

When the driving test has ended, you can call your instructor over if they didn't go with you on your test. This is so that they can listen to the result and your **feedback**. The examiner will tell you whether you passed or failed and will explain how you did during the test.

You will pass your test if your examiner has recorded fifteen or fewer driving faults and no serious or dangerous faults. Have a look at the following webpage if you are not sure what the difference is between a driving fault and a serious or dangerous fault.

Web wonders

www.direct.gov.uk/en/Motoring/
LearnerAndNewDrivers/PracticalTest/
DG_4022540

Where you can sit the test(s)

You can sit both your theory test and your practical test at any DSA approved test centre.

Motorcycles: Theory test

The theory test for motorcycle driving is exactly the same as for car driving, with a multiple choice part and a hazard perception part. Please see page 22.

Practical test

To pass the practical motorcycle test you need to pass its two separate modules within two years of passing your motorcycle theory test. Module one will test you doing set manoeuvres on the motorcycle in a safe off-road area. Module two is the on-road test.

You must provide all of the following valid documents:

- your driving licence with the correct provisional entitlement – both the photocard and counterpart document or a valid UK passport to support a paper licence
- your compulsory basic training (CBT) certificate (DL196)
- your motorcycle theory test certificate.

Module one currently includes the following specified manoeuvres and generally takes around 20 minutes to complete:

- wheeling the machine and using the stand

- doing a slalom and figure of eight
- cornering, hazard avoidance and controlled stop
- U-turn
- a slow ride
- the emergency stop.

There is a minimum speed requirement of 50 kilometres per hour (approximately 32 miles per hour) for the hazard avoidance and emergency stop exercises.

At the end of module one, the examiner will give you the result and feedback. If you passed, you'll receive your module one pass certificate.

For module two you must produce your module one pass certificate, and all the documents that you had to present at the module one test. Module two is the on-road module and typically takes around 40 minutes.

This module includes the

- eyesight test
- safety and balance questions
- road riding element that will cover a variety of road and traffic conditions
- independent riding.

You'll be asked to carry out

- normal stops
- an angle start (pulling out from behind a parked vehicle)
- a hill start (where possible).

The examiner will normally follow you on a motorcycle, using a radio to give you directions.

At the end of module two, the examiner will give you the result and feedback.

You can make up to ten rider faults and still pass module two. If you make eleven or more rider faults, you won't pass the module. If you make one serious or dangerous fault, you won't pass module two.

Where you can sit the test(s)
You can sit both your motorcycle theory test and practical test at any DSA approved test centre.

> **Write it down**
>
> Your friend Emma has heard you have just sat – and passed – your car driving test. She has emailed to ask you how much it cost, and what form the practical and theory tests took. Email her back with as much useful information as you can give her.
>
> OR
>
> Your friend Rav has heard you have just sat – and passed – your motorcycle driving test. He has emailed to ask you how much it cost, and what form the practical and theory tests took. Email him back with as much useful information as you can give him.

Outline the safety checks that should be carried out before using a vehicle

If your vehicle is over three years old, a mandatory requirement is that it has to pass an annual MOT test (see page 18 above). However, new cars and even cars which have passed the MOT should still be regularly maintained, and some basic safety checks carried out before you start a journey. Some basic safety checks for inside the car include the following:

- Doors – make sure that all doors are securely closed. Not only can they cause a distracting noise if not properly closed, they might open unexpectedly and cause an accident.
- Seating – having the seat in the correct position for you (so that you can operate all the pedals and other vehicle instruments) is an important part of journey preparation. It will ensure that you can keep proper control of the vehicle, it will keep you comfortable and it will help to reduce fatigue.
- Mirrors – they should be checked and adjusted before each journey to ensure that you have clear vision behind you.
- Steering – your steering position should be comfortable. Most modern cars allow you to adjust the steering column up and down to suit your needs.

- Seatbelt – this should be adjusted to ensure comfort when driving. Remember, it is the driver's responsibility to ensure that all passengers under the age of fourteen wear a seatbelt.

There are some further basic and simple safety checks that should be undertaken before you take any vehicle out onto the road:

- Fuel – check that you have sufficient fuel for your journey. If not, make sure that you fill up as soon as possible after you leave.

- Oil – check your oil levels, especially before a long journey, and top up if necessary. You can do this easily by checking the dipstick, which can be found under the bonnet.

- Brake fluid levels – these need to be checked to ensure that your brakes work correctly. If you find your brake fluid levels are changing you should get your brakes checked. Any significant change in fluid levels probably means there is a problem somewhere in the system.

- Electrics – make sure that all your electrics are in good working order. This particularly applies to lights and the horn. It is quick and easy to test these before each journey.

- Tyres – check the tread on your tyres to make sure that they are 'legal' to drive. There should be at least 1.6 mm of tread all round a car tyre. If the tyre is damaged in any way you should get it replaced – otherwise you may be a risk to yourself and other drivers. The rules for scooters are slightly different – make sure you know what they are.

- Tyre pressures – check these regularly and be sure to check them before a long journey. Check your vehicle manual for the correct pressures for both front and rear tyres.

Safety checks are essential and should be undertaken on a regular basis – and they are good preparation before any long journey. Remember, however, that many modern cars carry out these checks for you electronically. When you first get into a car that you don't know, make sure that you read the manual and find out what all the dashboard warning lights mean. These checks are just as important if you are riding a scooter or motorcycle.

For more information on vehicle maintenance, see page 69.

Did you know?

As part of your practical driving test you will be asked some vehicle safety questions. Here are some examples:

Table 1.4 Vehicle safety questions in the driving test

Question	Answer
Show me how you would check that the horn is working (off-road only).	Check is carried out by using the control (turn on **ignition** if necessary).
Open the bonnet, identify where the brake fluid reservoir is and tell me how you would check that you have a safe level of **hydraulic** brake fluid.	Identify reservoir, check level against high/low markings.
Show me how you would check that the direction indicators are working.	Applying the indicators or hazard warning switch and check functioning of all indicators. (You may need to switch ignition on.)
Show me how you would check that the brake lights are working on this car. (I can assist you; if you need to switch the ignition on, please don't start the engine.)	Operate brake pedal, make use of reflections in windows, garage doors, etc., or ask someone to help. (You may need to switch ignition on.)
Show me how you would clean the windscreen using the windscreen washer and wipers.	Operate control to wash and wipe windscreen (turn ignition on if necessary).

Information in 'The driving test' section is adapted from www.direct.gov.uk, © Crown Copyright.

In addition to vehicle safety checks, you should ensure that you are familiar with all aspects of the vehicle before starting your journey. This includes

- knowing and understanding the layout, instruments and controls of the vehicle you are about to use

- knowing where to look to identify the appropriate type of fuel for the vehicle, for example in the vehicle handbook or symbol on the fuel cap

- knowing how to familiarise yourself with a new vehicle, for example seating adjustments, instrument panel, gears, handling and brakes

- understanding the role of the reserve level indicator for low fuel (petrol/diesel)

- knowing where basic maintenance equipment is located and how it can be accessed if you break down.

End of Task test

Now complete the following multiple choice test.

1 You have third party insurance. What does this cover?

Select three

A Damage to own vehicle

B Injury to another person

C Damage to other vehicles

D Damage to your vehicle by fire

E Damage to someone's property

F Injury to yourself

2 To supervise a learner driver you must

Select two

A have held a full licence for at least three years

B be at least 21 years old

C be an approved driving instructor

D hold an advanced driving certificate.

3 You should contact the DVLA when you

Select three

A have changed your name

B have changed your vehicle

C have changed your job

D go on holiday

E change your address.

4 What is a SORN?

Select one

A A notification to VOSA that a vehicle does not have an MOT

B A notification to DVLA that a vehicle is not being used on the road

C Information held by the police about the owner of a vehicle

D Information held by insurance companies about the owner of a vehicle

5 An MOT certificate is normally valid for

Select one

A three years after the date it is issued

B one year after it is issued

C 15,000 miles

D 20,000 miles.

6 You have stopped at a pedestrian crossing and a disabled person is crossing slowly in front of you. The lights have changed to green. What should you do?

Select two

A Allow the person to cross

B Sound your horn

C Edge forward slowly

D Be patient

E Drive behind the person

F Drive in front of the person

7 You notice horse riders ahead. You should

Select one

A pull out to the middle of the road

B accelerate around them

C slow down and be ready to stop

D sound your horn to warn them you are near.

8 The left-hand pavement is closed due to street repairs. What should you do?

Select one

A Speed up to get past the roadworks more quickly

B Watch out for pedestrians walking on the road

C Position your vehicle close to the left-hand kerb

D Sound your horn as a warning

9 You are following a cyclist. You wish to turn left just ahead. You should

Select one

A overtake the cyclist before the junction

B hold back until the cyclist has passed the junction

C pull alongside the cyclist and tell him to cycle faster

D go around the cyclist at the junction.

10 Before starting a journey you should check your tyres to make sure

Select two

A they have not been stolen

B they are at the correct pressure

C they are not worn or damaged

D they are clean.

Unit 1 Understanding how to use the roads

Understand the road and use it safely

Identify key elements of the Highway Code

The Highway code is an important book for all road users as it outlines all the rules and regulations that pedestrians, animals, cyclists, motorcyclists and drivers should follow. In total there are 307 rules, along with information covering road signs, road markings, vehicle markings and road safety.

Many of the Highway Code's rules are legal requirements. Failure to follow these rules is classified as a criminal or civil offence and you can be fined, awarded penalty points on your driving licence or even banned from driving. Within the Highway Code, these rules are identified by the words **must** and **must not**.

Failure to follow the other rules of the Code (that is, those which say you should or should not do something) will not, in itself, cause a person to be prosecuted, but they are there to ensure road safety and as such should be followed.

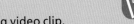

Web wonders

Watch the following video clip.

http://www.youtube.com/watch?v=C-U6c6w7Ap4&feature=channel

Attitudes

It is important to remember the following points:

- The Highway Code applies to EVERYONE who uses the roads, whether they are a pedestrian, riding a bicycle or a horse, driving a car or riding a motorcycle.
- The rules of the Highway Code must ALWAYS be followed.
- If you break the Highway Code there is a good chance that you will be caught and penalised.
- Following the rules of the Highway Code enables other road users to predict what you are likely to do.
- Failure to follow the rules of the Highway Code increases the chances that you will be involved in a crash.
- Knowing the rules that apply to you will help you be a better and safer driver or rider.
- If you feel that there are conflicts between the requirements of the Highway Code and other considerations then you probably do not really understand the Highway Code.
- Ignorance of the law of the road, as it applies to you, is NOT an excuse.

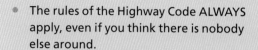
- The rules of the Highway Code ALWAYS apply, even if you think there is nobody else around.
- If you ever think 'Other drivers ignore the Highway Code, so why can't I?', remember that ignoring the Highway Code puts you and other road users at increased risk. It may also result in you being convicted and being fined or having your licence taken away.

Identify road types, junctions and pedestrian crossings and describe their functions

There are different types of roads in the UK.

Road types

Motorways are usually identified with an M on road signs, for example M25. These are high-speed roads where the maximum speed limit is 70 m.p.h. (110 km.p.h.). Motorways usually have a **hard**

shoulder at the left which is designed for use in emergencies or breakdowns. On some motorways you may find that you are directed to use the hard shoulder as another lane, for example, when traffic is very heavy. These roads are usually coloured blue on a road map.

Primary A roads are major routes which are not motorways. They can be either single or dual **carriageways** and are normally identified by an A on road signs, for example A90. The speed limit on these roads is usually 60 m.p.h. for a single carriageway and 70 m.p.h. for a dual carriageway (110 km.p.h.). Primary A roads tend not to have a hard shoulder. They are usually coloured green on a road map.

Non-Primary A roads are similar to the above but are less important routes. They are usually coloured red or orange on a road map.

B roads are less important roads, typically branching off of A roads and leading to smaller towns and villages. They are usually coloured brown or yellow on a road map.

Unclassified roads are local roads which have no defined destination.

Write it down

Study the road map below and answer the questions that follow.

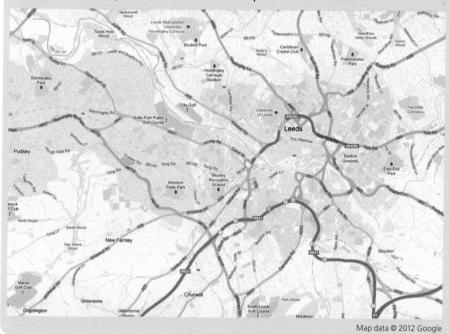

Map data © 2012 Google

1 Name two motorways shown on this map.

2 What is the name of the A road that goes through Pudsey?

3 How do you know that the A653, Dewsbury Road is a non-primary A road?

4 What is the name of the B road that would take you from Harehills Cemetery to Potternewton Park?

Road junctions

A road junction is a place where traffic from different directions meet. The junction is designed to allow traffic to move in a controlled manner in order to prevent accidents. This allows traffic to change routes and direction, if necessary.

Road junctions can appear simple and straightforward, such as this T junction.

Or they can be much more complex, such as this box junction.

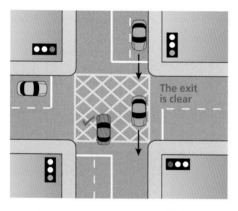

The exit is clear

Some junctions are controlled by traffic lights, some are directed by roundabouts, and others by road markings and road signs. No matter what the junction is, there are always a number of simple rules to follow:

- You need to give priority to other road users in some situations.
- If you are driving a car you need to keep an eye out for vulnerable road users such as pedestrians, cyclists and motorcyclists, as they might not be easy to see.
- If you are a pedestrian, a cyclist or a motorcyclist you need to think about how you make sure drivers see you.
- If you are driving and pedestrians are crossing a road into which you are turning, they have

priority and you should let them carry on crossing.

- If you are a pedestrian, you should be thinking about where traffic might be coming from and whether they will be able to stop if you decide to cross a road.
- It is important to remember that different sorts of vehicles will negotiate a junction in different ways. For example, a long, articulated lorry may move into the outside lane in order to turn left. Even then the back of their trailer may come very close to the kerb or even mount the pavement.

Web wonders

Watch the following video clips:

http://www.youtube.com/watch?v=Cr17Dv7wN9Q

http://www.youtube.com/watch?v=AKqZfbH8WNU

What general message are these clips trying to give?

There are road markings, road signs and methods of traffic control at nearly all junctions, all of which provide assistance or information to assist with safe road use.

The combination of the STOP road sign and the solid white line at this standard junction means that you must stop your vehicle and wait for a safe gap to emerge in the traffic before making a turn.

The combination of the GIVE WAY sign and the broken white line at this junction means that you need to give way to traffic when you are exiting this junction. It is not necessary to stop if there is a clear gap for you to move into.

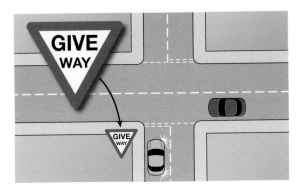

Particular care needs to be taken when crossing or turning onto any dual carriageway, especially when turning right.

Write it down

In the picture shown, explain why the lorry driver is making an incorrect movement when crossing the junctions on this busy dual carriageway.

Box junctions like the one below can be particularly difficult to cross. It is very easy for the junction to become totally clogged up with nobody able to move. To overcome this problem we sometimes use yellow box markings. You should not enter the yellow box unless your exit road or lane is clear of traffic. If you plan to turn right, you can enter the box and wait until there is a safe gap to make a turn.

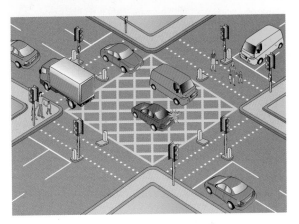

Some junctions are controlled by traffic lights. In these cases you should observe road markings and traffic light commands, such as a command to stop at the white line, unless the traffic light is set at green. If you have passed the white line when the traffic lights change to amber, you can continue your manoeuvre. Remember that the amber light also means STOP.

Pedestrian crossings

A pedestrian crossing is a designated place where pedestrians have the right of way to cross a road. There are different types of pedestrian crossings, but they all involve a means of stopping vehicles in order to ensure the safe crossing of a road. It is important that not only vehicle drivers, but pedestrians themselves know how to use each of these crossings correctly.

Currently, there are five types of controlled pedestrian crossing in the UK:

- Zebra
- Pelican
- Puffin
- Toucan
- Pegasus

Each of them is designed to let non-motorised road users cross busy roads safely.

A **pedestrian refuge** is the simplest form of crossing. This is usually in the form of an island in the centre of the road, as shown below.

Zebra crossings are safe crossing areas indicated by black and white painted stripes on the road, along with flashing amber lights/beacons. Drivers must give way when a pedestrian is stepping onto a zebra crossing. It is important, however, that pedestrians remember not to cross the zebra crossing until it is safe to do so: that is, when they are sure that a vehicle approaching the crossing is going to stop.

As a vehicle driver, when you approach a zebra crossing:

- You should watch out for pedestrians planning to cross and be ready to slow down or stop to let them cross.

- You **must** always give way when a pedestrian has stepped onto a crossing.

- In wet or icy conditions you should allow more time for stopping.

- You should not encourage pedestrians to cross by waving or using your horn; this could be dangerous if another vehicle is approaching.

- You should be aware of pedestrians approaching from the side of the crossing.

As a pedestrian you should remember that you must actually walk on the crossing. You cannot expect drivers or riders to stop if you try dashing across the road a few yards away from the crossing. Cyclists must also remember that the rules of a zebra crossing apply to them as well. You may not cycle across the crossing until pedestrians have stepped onto the pavement at the other side.

Pelican crossings are designed to give 'safe to cross' indications to both pedestrians and vehicle drivers. This crossing is operated by a pedestrian push button unit. Pelican crossings have red/amber/green signals facing drivers to tell them to prepare to stop, to stop or to go, and red man/green man signals on the opposite side of the road to the pedestrians waiting to cross. This crossing operates on the basis that:

- When the red man is lit pedestrians should not cross.

- When the steady red signal to traffic is lit, drivers **must** stop.

- The green man will then light for pedestrians and they should cross, having checked it is safe to do so.

- When the green man begins to flash pedestrians should not start to cross.

- Most pelican crossings have a bleeping sound to indicate to people with limited sight when the steady green man is lit.

At a pelican crossing, the flashing amber will always follow the red 'Stop' light. When the amber light is flashing, vehicles **must** give way to pedestrians. If the amber light is flashing and there are no pedestrians on the crossing, vehicles can carry on with caution.

The main difference between a **puffin** crossing and a pelican crossing is that puffin crossings do not have a flashing green man/flashing amber signal. The crossing is operated by a push button unit. Puffin crossings are smart: if someone presses the button but does not wait to cross, the system will cancel the request to cross, so that the traffic will not be stopped by a red light for no reason.

Note: Cyclists are not allowed to cross the road using zebra, pelican or puffin crossings.

Toucan crossings are specifically designed for use by both pedestrians and cyclists. For this reason they tend to be found in areas where there are cycle

paths. As well as showing the green man symbol they also show a green cycle symbol. As at puffin lights, at toucan crossings the crossing time is worked out each time by on-crossing detectors.

Pegasus crossings are similar to toucan crossings but are designed to allow crossing by horse riders. They are only found where horses and riders need to make many crossings across a busy main road. These crossings have a red/green horse symbol and higher mounted push buttons to allow horse riders to cross.

Note: At puffin, toucan and pegasus crossings, there is no flashing amber light for vehicles. Instead the light sequence for traffic is the same as at traffic lights.

Identify traffic signals, road signs and markings

Traffic signals

We are familiar with traffic light colours, red, amber and green, but we are perhaps not so familiar with their sequencing and in turn what this sequencing means.

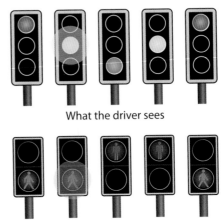

What the driver sees

What the pedestrian sees

Think it through

Match each of the signals below with the correct instruction. Use the Highway Code or other reference materials to help you with this task.

1 Stop and wait behind the stop line.

2 Wait behind the stop line and prepare to move off.

3 Continue ahead if the way is clear.

4 Stop at the stop line, unless doing so might cause an accident.

5 On a pelican crossing vehicles must give way to pedestrians if they are crossing, otherwise they can continue ahead.

6 Traffic going ahead must stop, traffic turning right can continue.

7 Traffic going right can continue.

Other signals

You will find lights being used to warn or give instructions at a number of other places in the road network.

At level crossings, airfields and fire stations, when you see a flashing red light you must stop. These crossings may or may not have barriers.

Motorway signals

These are illuminated signs that usually appear on overhead gantries (as shown in this illustration).

Some of them give instructions.

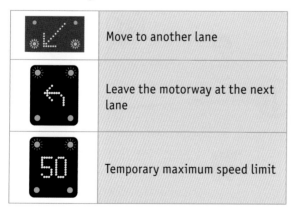

	Move to another lane
	Leave the motorway at the next lane
	Temporary maximum speed limit

Others give information.

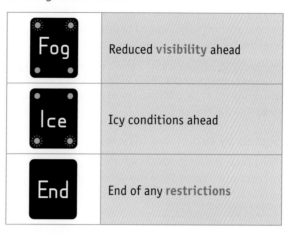

Fog	Reduced **visibility** ahead
Ice	Icy conditions ahead
End	End of any **restrictions**

Think it through

Find out what instruction or piece of information each of the following signs tell the motorist.

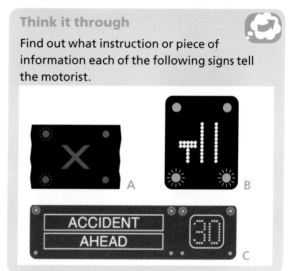

Other traffic signals

Remember that signals are not only things you find on the top of poles by the side of the road. Vehicles also give signals. Most vehicles have directional light indicators, brake lights, reversing lights and hazard indicator lights. These signal to other road users about a driver's **intentions**.

Think it through

What would cyclists use to indicate the following intentions?

1 I plan to turn left.
2 I plan to turn right.

You may also come across a variety of people who will signal to you (for example, to stop). Only certain people are normally allowed to direct traffic, for example, police, traffic wardens, school crossing patrol officers and officers from VOSA and the Highways Agency. The main signs that they will use are designed to stop traffic, make it change direction or to make it proceed.

Signals by authorised officials

The police, traffic wardens, school crossing patrol officers and officers from the Vehicle and

Operational Services Agency and Highways Agency all have authority to direct traffic. The basic controls are to stop traffic and to allow traffic to move forward, or prepare traffic to stop or move forward.

Think it through

Study each of the images below and identify what each signal is telling the road user to do.

A

B

C

D

E

F

G

H

I

J

Road signs

There are a large number of road signs used in the UK. They do a variety of jobs. They give the road user orders, warnings, instructions, information and directions.

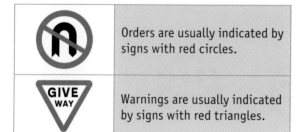

	Orders are usually indicated by signs with red circles.
	Warnings are usually indicated by signs with red triangles.

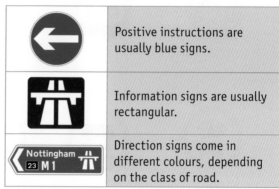

	Positive instructions are usually blue signs.
	Information signs are usually rectangular.
	Direction signs come in different colours, depending on the class of road.

Order signs

Think it through

Using the resources available to you, find out what each of the following order signs tell the road user.

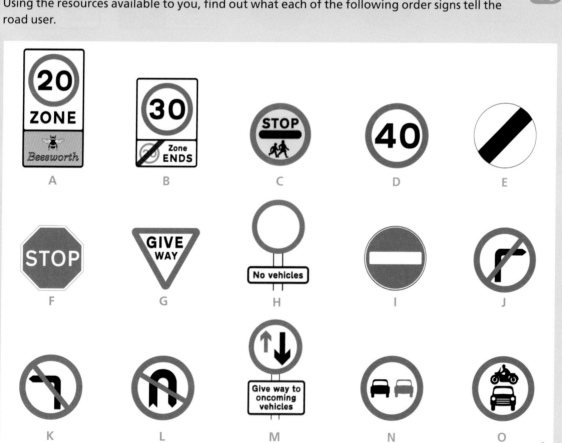

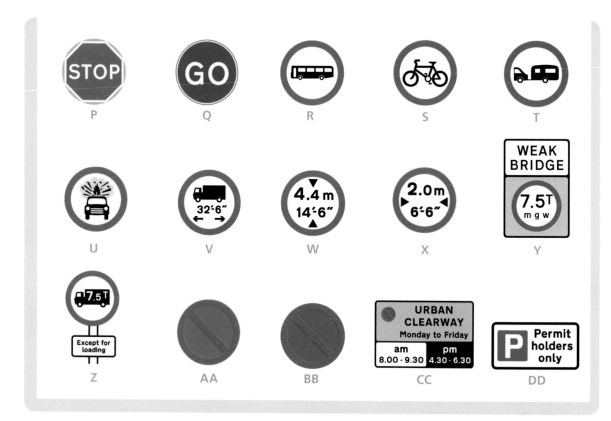

P   Q   R   S   T

U   V   W   X   Y

Z   AA   BB   CC   DD

Warning signs

The following signs provide the road user with a warning of a potential risk or danger. Some might not be obvious to the road user, such as the signs shown below:

Junction ahead controlled by a STOP sign

Junction ahead controlled by a GIVE WAY sign

Uneven road ahead

Two-way traffic crossing ahead

Side winds likely ahead

Electrified overhead cable ahead

Road narrows on the right ahead

Some road signs are more obvious to the road user.

Think it through

Match the following warning signs to the list of warnings provided.

U

V

W

X

Y

Z

AA

BB

CC

DD

EE

FF

GG

HH

II

JJ

KK

LL

MM

NN

OO

PP

QQ

RR

SS

Meanings

1 Tram crossing

2 Traffic signals

3 Two-way traffic straight ahead

4 Bend to right

5 Junction on bend ahead

6 Dual carriageway ends

7 Crossroads

8 Double bend, first to the left

9 Traffic signals not in use

10 Tunnel ahead

11 Level crossing without barrier

12 Steep hill upward

13 School crossing patrol

14 Zebra crossing

15 Traffic queues ahead

16 Pedestrians in road ahead

17 Sharp deviation to the left

18 Cattle

19 Wild animals

20 Accompanied horses

21 Soft verge for 2 miles

22 Ford

23 River bank ahead

24 T junction

25 Roundabout

26 Swing/open bridge ahead

27 Slippery road

28 Level crossing without gate/barrier

29 Road narrows both sides

30 Staggered junction

31 Low flying aircraft

32 Steep hill downward

33 Level crossing with gate/barrier

34 Reduce speed now

35 Falling rocks

36 Hidden dip

37 Frail/elderly persons crossing

38 Available width of headroom

39 Light signal ahead at level crossing/airfield

40 Wild horses

41 Cycle route

42 Risk of ice

43 Humps on road for ½ mile

44 Hump bridge

45 Risk of **grounding**

46 Junction on bend ahead

Directional signs

These signs are found on different types of roads and provide the road user with travel directions/locations.

Motorway signs are usually blue.

This sign is found on a motorway to confirm destinations. In this case the M1 leads to Sheffield, which is 32 miles away, and also to Leeds, which is 59 miles away.

This sign is found where a junction leads directly onto a motorway. In this case the junction is Number 23 and is leading to Nottingham. The motorway is called the M1.

41

This sign is found on the motorway to indicate an approaching junction. In this case junction 25 is half a mile away and leads to the A52 for Nottingham.

Think it through

What do the following signs tell the motorist?

Sign 1

Sign 2

Signs on primary routes (non-motorways) are usually green. They are found on approaches to junctions, at junctions and after junctions, just like those found on motorways.

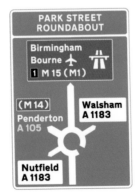

This sign is found at an approach to a junction – in this case a roundabout. The items in blue indicate that the junction leads to motorways. Where the

motorway is shown in brackets, this means that the motorway can be reached via this route. The aeroplane symbol indicates that an airport can be reached via this route.

On non-primary routes and local roads, signs are usually white with a black border (see below). The signs are found on approaches to junctions, at junctions and after junctions, like those found on motorways and primary roads.

Other direction signs vary in colour, from brown (indicating local tourist attractions) to blue (for example, routes for pedestrians or pedal cycles) or yellow (diversion signs).

Think it through

What information does this sign give the motorist?

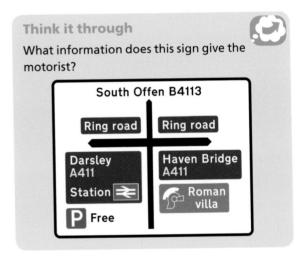

Information signs

Information signs are usually rectangular and can vary in colour. A few are shown below.

Start of motorway and point from which motorway regulations apply

Area in which cameras are used to **enforce** traffic regulations

Traffic has priority over oncoming vehicles

No through road for vehicles

Hospital ahead with Accident and Emergency facilities

End of motorway

Parking place for solo motorcycles

Advance warning of restriction or prohibition ahead

Motorway service area sign showing the operator's name

Tourist information point

Recommended route for pedal cycles

Appropriate traffic lanes at junction ahead

Countdown' markers at exit from motorway (each bar represents 100 yards to the exit)

Entrance to controlled parking zone

End of controlled parking zone

With-flow bus lane ahead which pedal cycles and taxis may also use

Bus lane on road at junction ahead

Roadworks signs

There are specific signs where there are roadworks in operation. These allow drivers to take care to ensure safety for all road users, including road workers.

Roadworks

Loose chippings

Roadworks 1 mile ahead

End of roadworks

Temporary hazard at roadworks

Temporary lane closure(s)

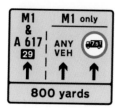

Lane restrictions at roadworks ahead

One lane crossover at contraflow roadworks

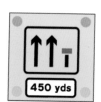

Signs used on the back of slow-moving or stationary vehicles warning of a lane closed ahead by a works vehicle. There are no cones on the road.

Slow-moving or stationary works vehicle blocking traffic lane. Pass in the direction shown by the arrow.

Mandatory speed limit ahead

Road markings

So far we have looked at signs and signals that are given by people, or signs that are found on different types of roads in the UK. All of these provide useful information for the road user. The roads themselves, however, also have markings that can assist safe road use.

Across the carriageway

These are road markings positioned across a road. The thickness, type and colour of line tell what the road marking means.

Stop line at signals or police control

Stop line at 'Stop' sign

Stop line for pedestrians at a level crossing

Give way to traffic on major road

Give way to traffic from the right at a roundabout

Give way to traffic from the right at a mini-roundabout

Along the carriageway

A broken white line in the middle of the road marks the centre of the road. When the broken line lengthens and the gaps shorten, it indicates a hazard ahead.

Double white lines, where the line nearest to you is broken, mean you can cross the lines to overtake if it is safe to do so. If the line nearest to you is solid, this means that you must not cross the line unless taking a right turn. Where both lines are solid, it means vehicles from either side must not cross the line.

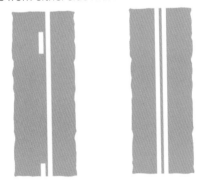

Diagonal stripes are there to separate lanes or protect traffic turning right. If the diagonal lines are surrounded

by a solid white line, you must not enter the diagonal lines. If surrounded by a broken line, you should still not enter unless it is safe and necessary to do so.

Edge lines indicate the edge of the road.

Short broken lines are used as lane dividers on wide roads. Vehicles should keep between these lines unless making a safe and legal manoeuvre.

Waiting and loading restrictions

Parked vehicles can be as much of a safety hazard as moving vehicles. It is for this reason that there are controls in place to limit where and when vehicles can park and load or unload. Markings are placed on the edge of the road to indicate what waiting and loading restrictions are in place.

Think it through

Using the resources available, find out what each of the following waiting or loading markings mean.

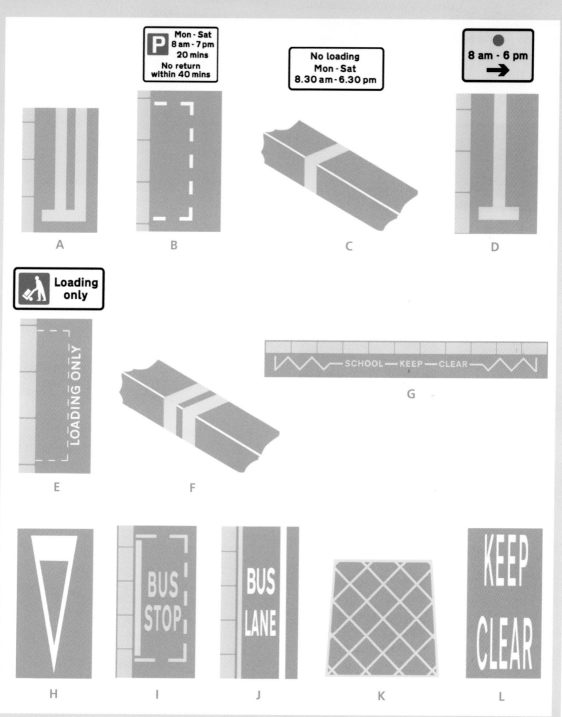

State the factors that affect a safe road speed

The ability to stop a vehicle at the correct place and the correct time is an important element of road safety. We have already seen that road signs, signals and markings can prepare us to stop our vehicle at the appropriate time. In order to be able to stop in time, you need to be observant and keep to the speed limit. It is for this reason that there are enforceable speed limits on all UK roads.

Speed limits

The following are the national speed limits in the UK.

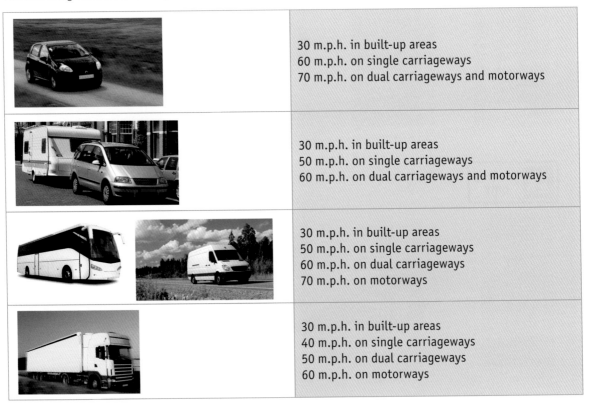

	30 m.p.h. in built-up areas 60 m.p.h. on single carriageways 70 m.p.h. on dual carriageways and motorways
	30 m.p.h. in built-up areas 50 m.p.h. on single carriageways 60 m.p.h. on dual carriageways and motorways
	30 m.p.h. in built-up areas 50 m.p.h. on single carriageways 60 m.p.h. on dual carriageways 70 m.p.h. on motorways
	30 m.p.h. in built-up areas 40 m.p.h. on single carriageways 50 m.p.h. on dual carriageways 60 m.p.h. on motorways

The above speed limits are provided in m.p.h. and are the maximum allowed on each road type for each vehicle, unless other road signs or signals tell you otherwise. Factors such as the weather, condition of the road, condition of the car, experience of the driver and so on need to be taken into consideration when judging what is a safe road speed. The maximum road speed limit is designed for when road conditions are good.

Think it through

Draw the road sign that you would see on a single carriageway which indicates a 60 m.p.h. speed limit.

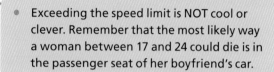
Did you know?

The 30 m.p.h. speed limit applies to all traffic on all roads with street lights, unless shown otherwise.

The national speed limit of 70 m.p.h. (dual carriageways and motorways) was first introduced in 1965.

Speed cameras were introduced in the 1990s and have succeeded in reducing the number of road accidents and deaths caused by speeding drivers.

Attitudes

It is important to remember the following points:

- Speed limits are NOT arbitrary.
- The probability that you will KILL somebody if you hit them at 30 m.p.h. is 7%. At 40 m.p.h. it is 31%.
- 2.5 seconds is the minimum amount of time it takes a driver or rider to react to a situation and apply the brake. In 2.5 seconds a vehicle doing 80 m.p.h. will travel nearly 100 yards.
- Speeding is NOT acceptable, no matter how technically competent you may think you are.
- The fact that the speed limit on some roads is 70 m.p.h. does NOT automatically mean it is safe to drive or ride at that speed. If there is ice or surface water on the road, for example, you may need to drive much more slowly.
- Whatever speed you are driving or riding at, you MUST be able to stop your vehicle safely. That may mean driving below the speed limit if traffic conditions require it.
- Speeding is often associated with aggressive driving. Aggression is an emotional state that can have a negative effect on your ability to make good decisions.

- Exceeding the speed limit is NOT cool or clever. Remember that the most likely way a woman between 17 and 24 could die is in the passenger seat of her boyfriend's car.

Speed cameras

Speed cameras are devices for identifying vehicles travelling over the legal speed limit. They can be fixed cameras at the side of the road, hand-held speed cameras, or police cameras which are attached to a police vehicle. Speed cameras are intended to be a means of reducing vehicle speed in areas of potential risk.

Write it down

Write a short article that could be included in a school magazine about the need for speed cameras as a mean of reducing road accidents.

Identify how different road users are affected by stopping distances

When driving in traffic, drivers and riders need to ensure that they can stop safely in order to react to any potential hazards or risks.

There are two important aspects to stopping distance: the thinking distance and the braking distance. There is an important difference between the two:

- Thinking distance is the distance a vehicle will travel between the moment the driver or rider sees a hazard and the moment they start to apply the brakes. At 20 m.p.h. the Highway Code suggests that a vehicle will travel 6 metres in this time. However, it is important to remember that the distance is only going to be this short in perfect conditions. In practice most people react much more slowly and it is probably safer to assume that a vehicle travelling at 20 m.p.h. will cover something like 20 metres before the brakes are applied.

- Braking distance is the distance a vehicle will travel between the moment the brakes are applied and the moment the vehicle comes to a stop. Again the Highway Code suggests that at 20 m.p.h. this distance is 6 metres. However, if the vehicle's brakes are not working as well as they should or if the road surface is slippery this distance could easily be doubled or trebled.

The overall stopping distance is calculated by combining the two.

> ### Think it through
>
> Explain why each of the following factors might affect stopping distance.
>
> 1 Weather
> 2 Road surface
> 3 Vehicle condition
> 4 Using a mobile phone

Table 1.5 Stopping distances

Speed (m.p.h.)	20	30	40	50	60	70	80
Thinking distance (metres)	6	9	12	15	18	21	24
Braking distance (metres)	6	14	24	38	54	75	96
Total stopping distance (metres)	12	23	A	53	B	96	C

> ### Think of a number
>
> What would be the stopping distances for A, B and C in Table 1.5?

> ### Did you know?
>
> There is a saying that goes 'Only a fool breaks the two-second rule.' This means that you should leave a two-second gap between you and the car in front.

There are a number of other factors that should be taken into account when determining the overall stopping distance, for example the type of vehicle, the age and condition of the vehicle, and aspects relating to the driver, such as health and age.

Stopping distance is badly affected by drink and drugs. Being under the influence of drink or drugs would reduce your ability to react quickly and so increase your stopping distance. Being tired would affect your stopping distance too.

The observation of stopping distances is an important part of safe road use. It ensures the safety of pedestrians crossing roads and junctions as well as other road users. The Highway Code tells us to be aware of vulnerable road users such as elderly drivers, people using mobile phones, and drivers with children in the car. These groups should be given more time, consideration and space.

> ### Attitudes
>
> It is important to remember the following points:
>
> - You have just as much chance as others of experiencing a negative road event (such as a traffic collision).
> - Driving needs your FULL attention.
> - It is NOT acceptable to answer phone calls when driving, even when stationary in traffic.
> - It is NOT acceptable to send OR read text messages when driving, even when stationary in traffic.

Identify how and where to leave a vehicle safely and securely

It is important that, if the driver or rider and passengers of any vehicle have to leave it, they do so safely, legally and securely. There are many reasons for this, including to prevent break-ins and theft, and ensuring you do not create a hazard for other road users, as well as for personal safety.

The most important reason is safety. You must make sure that leaving the vehicle does not, for example, involve stepping out into an oncoming stream of traffic or having to cross a busy road to reach your destination. You must also make sure that other road users do not have to swerve or change lanes to avoid your vehicle.

Most vehicle crimes are opportunistic, which means that the criminal tries vehicles where they see that the driver or rider has left doors unlocked or valuable objects in sight. Such vehicle crimes can be prevented by following some simple and sensible advice.

1 Secure your vehicle. Make sure that your doors and windows are locked when leaving the vehicle on its own. If you are leaving your crash helmet with your motorcycle or scooter, make sure it is in a lockable top box or pannier or is padlocked to the machine.

2 Never leave anything in view in your car, such as a briefcase or satnav. Lock them in the boot.

3 Never leave your keys in the vehicle, including spare keys.

4 30% of car crimes take place at night. If you have to park your vehicle at night, choose a well-lit place.

5 Never leave the engine running, for example, outside a petrol station, cash machine or shop. Remember that it is an offence to leave your vehicle running while unattended.

6 Close your car windows; open windows make car theft easier. But don't forget that if you leave an animal in a locked car you must leave them enough ventilation. The police may break into your car if they believe a dog, or other animal, is in distress because they are overheating.

There are other things you should think about when choosing a place to park your vehicle.

1 Look at the road markings and signs. Remember that road markings provide an indication of where you can and cannot park.

2 If you decide to use an off-road car park, choose one which is either security protected (for example by **CCTV**), or which has restricted entry and exit points.

3 If parking on the road, choose a place that is well-lit as it not only helps you get into your car but acts as a **deterrent** to car thieves.

4 Once in your car, drive away quickly with your doors locked.

5 Check vehicles round about you for anything suspicious.

Think it through

Find out information about vehicle anti-theft devices and services. This could include any of the following:

- alarm services
- remote keyless entry systems
- steering wheel locks
- tracking devices
- VIN etching
- immobilisers.

Attitudes

The following is a common attitude to road safety that we should try to correct:

- Once you get out of your car it is not your responsibility.

WRONG. You are responsible for your vehicle even when you are out of the car, for ensuring that it is parked legally and correctly, and that it does not present an obstacle or risk to other road users.

End of Task test A

Your next door neighbour has asked you to drop her eleven-year-old son off at school. You have agreed to take him to school, which is about a five-minute drive from your house.

1　Who is responsible for making sure that the eleven-year-old boy wears his seatbelt?

   A　You as the driver

   B　The boy as the passenger

   C　The parent of the boy who is the passenger

   D　It doesn't really matter if he wears a seatbelt

2　You are on the way to the school and you see the following sign:

What is this telling you?

   A　Pedestrians might be ahead

   B　Roadworks ahead

   C　Children crossing ahead

   D　Potholes ahead

3　You are approaching the school and you see the following sign with the light flashing amber. What does this sign tell you?

A　Drive with care

B　Temporary maximum speed limit of 20 m.p.h.

C　Temporary speed limit of 20 m.p.h. coming to an end

D　Temporary minimum speed limit of 20 m.p.h.

4　There is a school crossing patrol officer at the school. She is starting to raise her STOP sign. This tells you that you should

   A　prepare to stop

   B　stop

   C　speed up to pass her

   D　go.

5　On the way home it starts to rain heavily. A car overtakes you and pulls into the safe gap that you have left in front of you. You should

   A　flash your headlights and sound your horn

   B　try to overtake him

   C　slow down and regain a safe distance

   D　tailgate him.

End of Task test B

You are travelling to see a friend who lives 40 miles away. You have a satnav and mobile phone with you to help you get to your final destination. You will be using both the motorway and A roads.

1　When would be the best time to set your satnav for the journey?

   A　When you are en route

   B　Before you start the car engine

   C　Only when you think you are lost

   D　When you are driving and have a satellite link

2 You come across the following sign when travelling on an A road. What does this sign mean?

A Road accident two miles ahead

B Risk of grounding for two miles

C Hump back bridge for two miles

D Long vehicle two miles ahead

3 You see the following motorway sign. What action should you take?

A Leave the motorway at the next exit

B Move into the left-hand lane

C Only overtake vehicles using the left-hand lane

D Ignore the sign

4 You need to make a phone call to your friend for some directions. What is the safest way to use your mobile phone?

A Use a hands-free set

B Slow down when using it while driving

C Only use it on a straight stretch of road

D Find a suitable place to stop and then use the phone

5 What is the national speed limit on an A road?

A 30 m.p.h.

B 40 m.p.h.

C 60 m.p.h.

D 70 m.p.h.

Describe how to use the roads with regards to the Highway Code and other road users

The Highway Code is essential reading for all road users, whether pedestrians, cyclists, drivers of cars, buses or trucks, motorcyclists or horse riders. The rules that the Code contains may be legal requirements or they may be advisory. Either way, they represent the most up-to-date advice about how to use the roads safely. Knowing and applying the Code will help you to protect yourself and others and to reduce crashes and accidents. However, it only works if everybody abides by it.

It is important to keep up to date with any changes to the Highway Code that are taken into effect. It is a good idea to make sure to always keep a copy of the most recent printing of the Code. You might also want to have a look at the Highway Code's official Facebook or Twitter pages for regular tips and advice.

Describe the correct response to traffic signals, road markings, signals given by others and traffic control measures

The signals that we make as road users are designed to warn and inform other road users of what we plan to do and the movements we intend to make.

Pedestrians do not usually give signals. However, it is important to remember that, as pedestrians, you can also give other road users a clear indication of what you intend to do by things like where you stand on the pavement. It is also useful to try to make eye contact with drivers and riders and to acknowledge them if, for example, they slow down for you.

Whenever you do give a signal, you should

- ensure that it is clear and in plenty of time. Remember that it can be misleading to signal too early or too late
- use signals to inform other road users that you are about to change course or direction, stop or move off
- always cancel signals after you have completed the manoeuvre (if you are using indicators, for example)
- use hand or arm signals as well as your position on the road if you are a cyclist, as this will make your intentions clearer.

You should also

- watch out for signals given by other road users as they might affect the move that you intend to make
- remember that an indicator on another vehicle may not have been cancelled and so you need to be observant and watch for other indications of what they intend to do (for example, where they are positioning themselves on the road). If you are in any doubt, proceed with caution.

Remember that other people may use signals in a different way. For example, some lorry drivers from Europe may use their headlights to signal in a different way to UK drivers. Remember that somebody else signalling to you does not take away your responsibility to check for yourself whether it is safe to proceed.

You must obey signals given by

- police officers

- traffic officers
- traffic wardens
- school crossing patrols.

If the police need to stop your vehicle they will
usually let you know by

- using flashing blue lights, headlights or sounding
  their siren or horn, or a combination of all three,
  usually from behind
- instructing you to pull over to the side of the
  road, or to a safe stopping place, by pointing
  and/or using the left indicator.

When instructed to do so, you **must** pull over and
stop as soon as it is safe to do so and switch off
your engine.

Vehicle & Operator Services Agency Officers are also
able to stop vehicles on all roads, although they are
usually interested in lorries and trucks. They will let
you know that they wish you to stop by

- flashing amber lights from the front instructing
  you to follow them to a safe place to stop
- flashing amber lights from behind, instructing
  you to pull over to the side of the road, or to a
  safe stopping place, by pointing and/or using the
  left indicator.

It is an offence not to comply with their instructions.

You must obey all traffic light signals and traffic signs
giving orders, including **temporary** signals and
signs. So it is important that you know, understand
and are able to obey and follow all traffic and
information signs and road markings.

You should only use your vehicle horn when your
vehicle is moving, and then only when you need to
warn other road users that you are there. You should
never use your horn to let other drivers know that
you are annoyed by the action that they have taken!
You must not use your horn

- while not moving on the road
- when driving in a built-up area between the
  hours of 11.30p.m. and 7.00a.m., unless it is to
  alert another road user to a possible danger.

Describe what to do if you are in a vehicle that breaks down

If your vehicle breaks down, it is important that you
take steps to ensure the safety of yourself and other
road users.

Breaking down on a road with no hard shoulder

1 If possible, try to get your vehicle off the road as
   quickly as possible to avoid obstructing traffic –
   but do not put yourself or your passengers at risk.

2 Switch on your hazard warning lights. Make sure
   your sidelights are on if visibility is poor.

3 If you think your car might be in danger of being
   hit by another vehicle, leave the vehicle and move
   to a safe place well away from the road. This is
   particularly important on motorways or fast dual
   carriageways.

4 Put up a warning triangle (if you have one) 45
   metres behind your car. It is important that you
   take care when placing or retrieving the warning
   sign. These should never be used on a motorway.

5   Call a breakdown or recovery service.

6   Do not stand between your vehicle and oncoming traffic. This also applies to any passengers in your vehicle.

7   At night or in poor visibility position yourself where you will not prevent other road users seeing your lights.

Breaking down on the motorway or dual carriageway

If your vehicle appears to be developing a problem (for example, if one of the warning lights comes on), leave the motorway at the very next exit or pull into a service area. If you are unable to do any of these, then you should:

1   Pull over onto the hard shoulder. The wheels of your car should be turned to the left.

2   If you don't have a mobile phone, emergency phones are usually situated at approximately one mile intervals along the hard shoulder of a motorway. Stop near an emergency phone if possible.

3   Switch on the sidelights and hazard lights.

4   Use the emergency phone on your side of the motorway to phone for help. Emergency phones are free of charge and are better than a mobile phone, because the police will be able to identify your location easily.

5   If you cannot see an emergency phone you should look for one of the blue and white marker posts by the side of the hard shoulder. These usually have an arrow pointing to the nearest phone. If you do not want to leave your vehicle, and you use your mobile phone to call the emergency services, you should tell them the number printed on the marker post. This will tell them exactly where you are. Some motorways also have larger blue signs giving similar information every 500 metres or so.

6   Leave the vehicle by the left-hand door, making sure that your passengers do the same.

7   Wear a reflective jacket if you have one.

8   Any animals should be kept in the vehicle unless there is an emergency such as fire. If you have to release the animal because of such an emergency, make sure that the animal is not able to escape and run onto the motorway.

9   Do not put yourself in danger for any reason, for example by trying to carry out roadside repairs.

10 Wait on the far side of the vehicle, climbing halfway up the bank if possible.

11 If for any reason you feel at risk from another person, then you should return to your vehicle immediately, using the left-hand door, and lock all doors.

Web wonders

Watch the following video clip:

http://www.youtube.com/ watch?v=lgqqnbyLhrg

Write it down

Look again at some of the points about breaking down on the motorway. Explain the importance of the parts highlighted in bold.

A   Pull over onto the hard shoulder. **The wheels of your car should be turned to the left.**

B   **Stop near an emergency phone if possible.**

C   **Switch on the sidelights and hazard lights.**

D   Leave the vehicle **by the left-hand door,** making sure that your passengers do the same.

E   **Wait on the far side of the vehicle, climbing halfway up the bank if possible.**

Describe what to do if you are involved in, or are a witness to, an incident

What should you do if you become involved in a road accident?

> **Web wonders**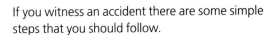
>
> Watch the following video clip:
>
> http://www.youtube.com/
> watch?v=w0cGKYZZz_k

If you witness an accident there are some simple steps that you should follow.

Stay calm

Try not to panic, as this will not help you to think rationally. If you panic you may make matters worse and cause risk to other road users.

Understandably, this is not always easy to do. If you feel yourself panicking, try turning away and taking four or five long, slow breaths. Count to ten, say a nursery rhyme, sing a few lines of your favourite song or do something to interrupt the panic, then turn round and focus on doing one thing at a time.

Inform the emergency services

- If you think the accident requires the emergency services, dial 999 as quickly as possible. If you are not able to call 999, get a passenger or a witness to do so.
- Check on any injured people and let the emergency services know the extent of the injuries.
- The emergency services will probably ask you to provide them with more details about the accident, including
  - the location of the accident
  - the number of casualties
  - the extent of their injuries
  - potential dangers
  - whether anyone is trapped inside a vehicle.
- Remain at the accident scene until you have spoken to a police officer – they may require a witness statement from you.

- It is important to remember that all vehicles involved in an accident are required to stop so that they can exchange details for insurance purposes.
- If you spot a vehicle which was involved in an accident driving away from the accident scene, make a note of the registration number and pass it on to the police.

Warn other drivers

- Use your hazard warning lights to warn traffic about the situation ahead.

Deal with casualties

- Do not move anyone who is injured unless you have been told to do so by the emergency services, or it is absolutely vital to do so, for example, if the vehicle is on fire or you see fuel leaking which you think might catch fire. If you can do so safely, make sure that the ignition on each vehicle is switched off.
- Try to make casualties as comfortable as possible, without moving them unnecessarily.
- Don't give an injured person anything to eat or drink, just in case they later need medical assistance.
- It is illegal to move a vehicle that has been involved in an accident or to remove debris from an accident scene.

First aid

- First aid can be applied to casualties by qualified first aiders, while waiting for medical help to arrive.
- Apply direct pressure to bleeding wounds and if you are sure there are no other problems, such as broken bones, raise the affected part of the body to limit bleeding – as long as you know what you are doing!
- Do not move anyone if you suspect they have a broken or fractured bone.
- If possible keep casualties warm by covering with a blanket.
- Treat burns buy pouring over cold water, ideally for at least 20 minutes. This might not always be possible.
- If you don't think you know what to do to treat a casualty, then don't attempt it!

Did you know?

The first few minutes after any accident are critical. If you are able to apply even the most basic first aid you may be able to make the difference between somebody living or dying. You may also be able to prevent their injuries becoming worse. You can get training in basic first aid from the St John's Ambulance or the Red Cross. It will only take you a few hours but you may save a life.

Avoid smoking

- Do not smoke near an accident scene. There may be leaking fuel which could ignite and make the situation worse.

Write it down

Using the resources available, including the Internet, write a short report for the school magazine which tells other students what they should do if they are involved in a road accident. Use the following headings to help you:

- What should I do?
- What happens when I report the collision?
- Do I have to make a statement?
- What do I do if the other driver wasn't insured?
- Should I contact my insurance company?
- Can I get the other driver's details from the police?
- Will I be prosecuted?
- My car is damaged. What happens next?

Attitudes

It is important to remember the following points.

- Car insurance is ALWAYS necessary.
- It's NOT OK to give someone first aid if you have no first aid training – it may do more harm than good.
- If you have had some training and you act in good faith you will not be penalised if you apply that training to the best of your ability.

The following are common attitudes which we should try to correct.

- It is better not to get involved in another road user's accident or incident.
- If the accident was not my fault, it is not my responsibility to get involved.

If you witness a road accident, even if you are not directly involved, you can be very important to those who are involved, by summoning aid if people are injured and helping the emergency services to understand how the accident happened.

End of Task test

1 Your vehicle breaks down in a tunnel. What should you do?

Select one

A Stay in front of your vehicle and wait for the police

B Stand in the lane behind your vehicle to warn others

C Stand in front of your vehicle to warn oncoming drivers

D Switch on hazard light and call for help immediately

2 You break down on a level crossing. The lights have not yet begun to flash. Which **three** things should you do?

Select three

A Phone the signal operator

B Leave your vehicle and get everyone clear

C Move the vehicle if the signal operator tells you

D Walk down to the track and signal to the oncoming train

E Tell the drivers behind that you are stuck

3 Your tyre bursts while you are driving. Which **two** things should you do?

Select two

A Pull on the handbrake

B Pull up slowly at the side of the road

C Continue at normal speed

D Brake as quickly as possible

E Hold the steering wheel firmly to keep control

4 Your vehicle has a puncture on a motorway. What should you do?

Select one

A Drive slowly to the next service area to get assistance

B Switch on your hazard lights and stop in your lane

C Pull onto the hard shoulder and change the wheel as quickly as possible

D Pull onto the hard shoulder and use the emergency phone to get assistance

5 You are on a motorway. When can you use hazard warning lights?

Select two

A When driving on the hard shoulder

B When you slow down quickly because of a danger ahead

C When a vehicle is following too closely

D When you are towing another vehicle

E When you are broken down on the hard shoulder

6 A collision has just happened. An injured person is lying in a busy road. What is the **first** thing you should do to help?

Select one

A Treat the person for shock

B Warn other traffic

C Make sure the injured person is kept warm

D Place them in the recovery position

7 There has been a collision. A motorcyclist is lying injured and unconscious. Unless it's essential, why should you usually **not** attempt to remove their helmet?

Select one

A They will get cold

B You could scratch the helmet

C It could result in further injury

D They might not want you to

8 At the scene of a traffic incident you should

Select one

A leave vehicle engines switched on

B go to the casualties that are screaming out loud

C pull everyone from their vehicles

D not put yourself at risk.

Developing positive road user attitude

Explain how attitudes of yourself and others can affect safe road use

Identify own relevant characteristics

A characteristic is a trait, feature, distinguishing quality or an attribute of an individual that makes that person distinctive. Your characteristics can affect road safety for yourself and others. Other people's characteristics can make you react and feel in certain ways that will also affect road safety. Generally these characteristics can be expressed as having a positive (good) or a negative (bad) effect on a person.

Think it through

The chart below identifies some positive and some negative characteristics. There are some blank spaces in the chart which you have to complete.

Table 2.1 Positive and negative characteristics

Positive characteristics	Negative characteristics
respects authority, loyal, devoted	rebellious
accepts what's given	ignores, rejects what's given
aspiring, ambitious, motivated	self-satisfied, unmotivated
	uncaring, unfeeling
accepts/welcomes change	rejects change
cheerful	
considerate, thoughtful	inconsiderate, thoughtless
co-operative	uncooperative, unhelpful
courageous	cowering, fearful
	rude, impolite
decisive	indecisive
determined	indecisive, unsure

Positive characteristics	Negative characteristics
does what is necessary, right	does what is convenient
perseveres, endures	
has faith in others	thinks others can't be relied on
flexible	inflexible, rigid, unbending, stubborn
forgiving	unforgiving, resentful, spiteful
focused	unfocused, scattered
friendly	
frugal, thrifty	wasteful, spendthrift
grateful	ungrateful, unappreciative
honest	dishonest, deceiving, lying
humble	arrogant, conceited, egocentric

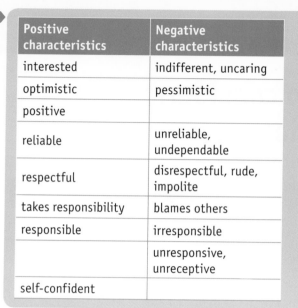

Positive characteristics	Negative characteristics
interested	indifferent, uncaring
optimistic	pessimistic
positive	
reliable	unreliable, undependable
respectful	disrespectful, rude, impolite
takes responsibility	blames others
responsible	irresponsible
	unresponsive, unreceptive
self-confident	

Positive characteristics	Negative characteristics
sensitive	
sympathetic	unsympathetic, unfeeling
organised	unsystematic, disorganised, disorderly, random
takes others' point of view	insists on own view
thoughtful towards others	
unselfish	selfish

What is important to remember about the characteristics of a person is that even those characteristics that are classed as positive can in fact have a negative effect on road safety and vice versa.

Think it through

Thinking about yourself, list two positive and two negative characteristics that you think apply to you and then explain the effect that each might have on road use and road safety.

Now ask a family member or a friend to identify four characteristics that they might use to describe you. Were you surprised by any of the characteristics that they identified? If so, why were you surprised?

Sometimes, when we are under stress, we can display characteristics that we might not recognise or associate with ourselves. The common expression is that 'he acted out of character'. Stressful situations can also lead to road accidents because we act in a manner that is different.

As well as characteristics, we need to think about a person's attitude, which can also affect road safety. An attitude is a person's like or dislike for something – it could be a person, a thing or an event. Attitudes are judgements that affect your behaviour, responses and thinking.

Attitudes

Look at the list of common attitudes of some young people to aspects of road safety and decide whether they are right or wrong.

- The Highway Code doesn't apply to you.
- Driving over the speed limit is exciting.
- It's fine to drive without car insurance.
- You become a safer driver with old age.
- Driving under the influence of alcohol has little effect on safe road use.
- Having passengers in your car can make you a better driver.
- Driving fast can reduce time pressure.

Answer: All of these attitudes are WRONG, can contribute to unsafe road use and endanger those around you.

Think it through

List three other attitudes of road users that might have a negative effect on road safety.

63

Identify key factors to consider before setting out on a road journey

We have looked at how attitudes can affect road safety, and earlier in the book we looked at factors that can affect road safety and at how you would decide if you and your companions were fit to travel.

- Having passengers in the car does NOT necessarily make you more alert.
- Having passengers in the car does NOT make you a better driver.

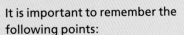

Attitudes

It is important to remember the following points:

- Cannabis does NOT reduce aggression and does NOT make you a better driver.
- Driving when under the influence of alcohol or illegal drugs always has a NEGATIVE effect on crash involvement and severity.
- You DO need to know the safe limits of alcohol consumption – these limits apply to YOU.
- Drinking coffee, winding down the window or listening to music will NOT reduce fatigue.
- Fatigue does NOT only occur on long journeys, or mainly on country roads.
- Fatigue IS a contributor to serious crashes.
- There ARE consequences for fatigued driving (the police can detect a fatigued driver).
- The assumption that most fatigue-related crashes occur at night is WRONG.
- Driving when suffering from fatigue is JUST as dangerous as driving when drunk or speeding.
- Your friends' expectations should NOT influence your own behaviour. →

Identify the risks and responsibilities of carrying passengers, animals and goods

There are certain risks and responsibilities associated with having passengers, animals and goods in your car. Let's look at each in turn.

Passenger numbers

In order to ensure the safety of a vehicle's passengers, it is the responsibility of the driver not to have more passengers than the maximum number the car is designed to carry. The maximum number of passengers is determined by the number of seatbelts in the car or vehicle.

Technically, it is legal to allow rear seat passengers to travel without a seatbelt if there are not enough seatbelts in the car, but this can be dangerous. It has been known for passengers sitting in the front seat to be killed or severely injured if an unrestrained rear seat passenger is launched into the back of the front seat in the event of an accident. Because of this, you should avoid carrying passengers if there is no seatbelt available for them to use.

If you are riding a scooter or motorcycle and you want to carry a pillion passenger, the vehicle must be fitted with a proper seat and footrests. Any person riding on the pillion must be able to reach the footrests and hold on securely.

Seatbelts

All drivers are legally **obliged** to ensure that all passengers who are under the age of fourteen wear a seatbelt. For passengers under the age of three, there are also specific requirements: the child must be suitably restrained by a booster seat, a car seat or a baby harness. These should carry a **BS Kitemark** or an **E mark** and be suitable for the weight of the passenger. It is illegal to carry a child in a rear-facing seat fitted in the front seat of a car which is protected by an active frontal airbag, as this may cause serious injury or the death of the child. However, many cars are fitted with switches that allow the driver to switch off the passenger seat airbag. Some car manufacturers also produce baby seats which are specially designed to fit into their cars and to switch off the airbag when fitted.

Children must be secured in both the front and back seats in a suitable child **restraint** until they are twelve years old or taller than 135 cm in height. Correct child restraints must be used where seat belts are fitted in the back of a vehicle. If a child aged three or over is travelling in a licensed taxi or private hire vehicle, or they have to be carried over a short distance for an unexpected reason and an appropriate child restraint is not available, they must use the adult seat belts. Adult seatbelts should be worn by children over the age of twelve or who are above 135 cm in height.

For passengers aged fourteen and above, it is their personal responsibility to wear a seatbelt.

If you are caught not wearing a seatbelt you can be given a fixed penalty fine of £60 but you will not have penalty points added to your licence. If you are convicted of an offence and you do not accept a fixed penalty you can be fined up to £500.

Did you know?

You're twice as likely to die in a crash if you are not wearing a seatbelt.

Web wonders

Watch the following video clips about the impact of not wearing a seatbelt:

http://www.youtube.com/watch?v=sL5-L8NS5zk

http://www.youtube.com/watch?v=g-9JR2P4wWI

Think it through

Using the web link below, try the crash simulator for the following situation.

http://think.direct.gov.uk/seat-belts.html

- Car type 1
- Male and female adult and one male child
- Two adults in front and child in back
- All are not wearing seatbelts
- Speed at 40 m.p.h.

What were the consequences for the people in the car?

Repeat the exercise but with all the people wearing seatbelts. What is the main difference?

Repeat the original exercise but with the speed at 20 m.p.h. What is the main difference?

Table 2.2 Summary of the seatbelt laws for cars, taxis and private hire cars

	Front seat	Rear seat	Who is responsible?
Driver	Seatbelt **must** be worn if available.		Driver
Children under 3 years old	Correct child restraint **must** be used.	Correct child restraint **must** be used. If one is not available in a taxi, then the child may travel unrestrained in the rear.	Driver
Children aged 3 and above, until they reach **either** their 12th birthday **or** 135 cm in height	Correct child restraint **must** be used.	Where seatbelts fitted, correct child restraint **must** be used. **Must** use adult belt if the correct child restraint is not available in three scenarios: in a licensed taxi or private hire vehicle; for a short distance for reason of unexpected necessity; two occupied child restraints prevent fitment of a third. In addition, a child 3 and over may travel unrestrained in the rear seat of a vehicle if seatbelts are not available.	Driver
Children over 135 cm, or 12 to 13 years	Seatbelt **must** be worn if available.	Seatbelt **must** be worn if available.	Driver
Adult passengers (i.e. 14 years and over)	Seatbelt **must** be worn if available.	Seatbelt **must** be worn if available.	Passenger

Source: **http://www.childcarseats.org.uk/law/**

Think it through

Answer the following questions:

1 Whose responsibility is it to ensure that a seatbelt is being worn by a person over the age of fourteen?

2 Why is it illegal to allow a child seat to face backwards if you have front airbags in your car?

3 Who has responsibility for ensuring that a child under the age of fourteen is wearing a seatbelt?

4 What is important about the height 135 cm?

5 What are the financial penalties of not wearing a seatbelt?

The risk associated with carrying passengers

People might say that having passengers on board a vehicle might help to combat boredom and tiredness and can even be helpful in terms of navigating and map reading. However, let's consider other aspects of carrying passengers which could impact negatively on your ability to drive safely and responsibly.

Passengers can cause **distraction** if:

- they talk, shout, argue, or laugh among themselves or with you. This will reduce your ability to react to situations
- they have music on too loud
- you have to deal with behaviour problems of passengers.

If these risks exist in cars, just think how much more of a problem a disruptive pillion passenger would be.

Web wonders

Watch the following video clip about passenger distractions:

http://www.wonderhowto.com/how-to-drive-safely-when-you-have-distracting-passengers-383747/

Passengers who are under the influence of either drugs or alcohol can be a distraction and may cause risk to the driver and other road users. You should be able to take appropriate action to prevent this risk.

It has been estimated that there are thousands of incidents of driver distraction caused by drunk passengers over the festive period in the UK, and a road accident can be a consequence. Some of the causes of distraction are:

- the passenger feeling ill and being sick
- the passenger being boisterous and singing loudly
- the passenger turning up the radio too loud
- the passenger interfering with the driving process, for example by pulling the handbrake or tugging the steering wheel
- all of these together.

> **Think it through**
>
> What should you do, as a driver, in these situations where you are being distracted by passengers?

Carrying animals

When transporting animals in a vehicle it is important that they are secured – not only to save the animal being injured as a result of an accident, but also to prevent the animal itself causing an accident, for example by jumping onto the driver's knee. At 30 m.p.h., a 22.5 kg dog would be thrown forward with a force equivalent to almost nine 76 kg men. The rules that apply to carrying passengers equally apply to animals – as we can see below.

Animals that are not secured in a moving vehicle can be a safety risk. Sudden movement or sound in the vehicle may cause an unrestrained animal to move about the vehicle and cause a distraction to the driver, resulting in an accident. An unfastened animal may escape from a vehicle and become a hazard to other road users.

Animals and pets must be safely secured in

- a seatbelt harness
- a pet carrier, behind a dog guard

- a dog cage
- a suitably well-ventilated zip-up bag – but only in emergency situations!

The most suitable restraint will depend on the needs of your pet.

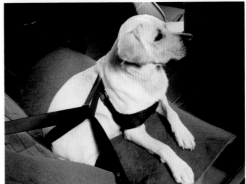

Other tips for transporting animals include the following:

1 Do not let your pet stick its head out of an open window. It can be a distraction for other road users as well as being a danger to the animal itself: for example, flies and other insects can hit the animal's eyes.

2 If you have airbags in your vehicle, position the animal in a place where, if inflated, the airbags cannot cause crushing or suffocation.

3 If you have pet insurance, check to see that it covers injury in a car accident.

4 If you have to leave your animal for a short time in the car alone (which is not advised), make sure the car is parked out of direct sunlight and is well ventilated. Leave a window partly open.

Carrying goods in your vehicle

Sometimes we need to use our cars to carry large items, such as suitcases for a holiday, or furniture we have bought, or garden waste we are taking to the recycling centre. What is important is that these goods are securely packed so that they do not become a road safety issue. Sometimes people try to do the same thing on a motorcycle or scooter. Take some time to think about why it is even more dangerous to carry large or heavy loads on a two-wheeled machine.

When carrying large or heavy items, your car has to cope with additional weight. In this case you should ensure the correct tyre pressure – check your vehicle owner's manual for the correct pressures.

This also applies to using a roof rack or roof storage box, but remember that because these are positioned on the top of your car they can affect the drag and balance of your car.

Before starting a journey where you will be carrying goods, you need to make sure that the objects in the car are secured well enough to prevent them from moving around and getting damaged or distracting you while you are driving. It is important that you do not try to store items in places that might hinder your ability to drive safely: for example, do not put anything in the driver's foot area, because if you brake suddenly these items may slide forward and could get under your pedals, which could cause a serious accident.

Think about visibility as you load up your car, making sure that you still have maximum visibility and that your view of the mirrors is not affected. A general rule is that everything should be stacked below shoulder level.

When driving a heavily packed vehicle it is important to drive more slowly than usual, as the added weight can drastically affect braking distances and your handling in corners.

If you have an item on a roof rack, make sure that it is well secured. If it falls onto the road, it could cause a serious accident. In such cases, you would need to try to safely retrieve the items from the road or contact the emergency services to let them know of the situation.

Lots of people like to go touring on their bicycles. They carry their tents, sleeping bags, cooking equipment and spare clothing with them in specially designed panniers or saddle bags. If you are riding a heavily loaded bicycle you need to recognise that you cannot pull away as quickly and you may be less manoeuvrable. Other road users need to understand that a heavily loaded cyclist needs to be given extra time and space.

It is possible to carry loads on a motorcycle or scooter but the limits to what you can carry are much more **stringent**. It is possible to buy panniers or top boxes to fit many sorts of scooter and motorcycle and these are specially designed to distribute the load in the safest possible way. If you do carry heavy loads, for example, if you go touring, you must check your handbook and make sure you make any necessary adjustments to the suspension or to tyre pressures. You must also be aware that the handling characteristics of your machine, for example, the stopping distance or the ease with which it turns, may be changed.

Think it through

Would you say that the luggage in the above cartoon is safely secured?

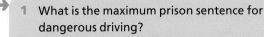

Identify the legal requirements for travelling using a vehicle

Before starting a journey, as well as carrying out the basic vehicle safety checks mentioned earlier (page 24), you need to ensure that all your vehicle documentation is valid and up to date:

1 Make sure that documentation relating to yourself as a driver or rider and to your vehicle meets legal requirements.

2 Make sure that your driving licence is valid for the category of the vehicle you are driving.

3 Make sure that you have valid insurance for your vehicle and for the circumstances in which you intend to use it.

4 Make sure that your vehicle registration and vehicle tax are up to date and that the tax disc is displayed properly.

5 Make sure that the vehicle has a current MOT certificate (where applicable).

Breaking the law and penalties

If you break the rules and regulations of the road, you can be stopped by the police or other enforcement agents and be charged. The charge could result in

- being given a fixed penalty fine, for example for not wearing a seatbelt
- being given a fixed penalty **endorsement**, that is, a cash fine and points added to your licence (for example, for not stopping at a red light)
- being taken to court and having a larger fine, prison sentence and disqualification imposed and in some cases your vehicle impounded.

→

1 What is the maximum prison sentence for dangerous driving?

2 What is the current Fixed Penalty Notice fine for speeding offences?

3 What is the current Fixed Penalty Notice points endorsement for speeding offences?

4 What is the maximum fine for dangerous cycling?

5 What are the penalties for driving without insurance?

Identify why it is important to carry out regular vehicle safety maintenance

Regular vehicle maintenance is an important factor in ensuring that your vehicle does not break down and that it lasts for a long time. The owner's manual for your vehicle is a great starting point for tips on routine simple maintenance. If you don't want to check your vehicle yourself, take it to your local garage and have them check everything – once a month would be suitable for routine checks on tyres, oil, other fluid levels, and so on. You will be charged for these checks, so it is a good idea to learn how to do them yourself. Of course, you should follow the vehicle's recommended service plan to make sure that any vehicle **warranties** are protected.

Tyres

- Know the correct tyre pressures for your front and rear tyres and check on a regular basis (every two weeks). Inflate as necessary.

- Recommended pressure figures as provide in vehicle handbooks are for cold tyres, so you'll get a higher reading if you check them after driving for more than a few minutes. Always check tyre pressures cold if possible.

- Tyre pressure can be measured in p.s.i. (pounds per square inch) or Bar (1 Bar is roughly the equivalent to atmospheric pressure). All garage

Think it through

Visit the following website and answer the questions that follow:

http://www.drivingban.co.uk/
drivingoffencespenalties.htm →

air devices use this same measurement. Your vehicle handbook will give you the correct p.s.i. or Bar for your vehicle's front and rear tyres.

- If the amount on the pressure gauge is below that mentioned in the owner's manual, the tyre will need to be inflated.
- If too much air is put into the tyre, you should let some out by depressing the pin in the centre of the valve.
- Look for cuts on the sides of the tyre. If a tyre needs regular top-ups of air, it may have a slow puncture. Take it to a garage to be checked.
- Remember to check your spare tyre – if you have one in your vehicle – at the same time as your other tyres.
- Some tyres are 'run flats' so you will not have a spare tyre. Look at your vehicle manual for specific instructions.

Don't forget to check the tyre pressures on your bicycle. If they are too soft it will be much harder to ride. Of course, if you are doing off-road riding you may want soft tyres for a particular reason but you need to think about whether the pressure is still right when you go back on the road.

Web wonders

Watch the following video clip:

http://www.youtube.com/watch?v=THX9dymm9zM

Toolkit

- Most cars, scooters and motorcycles will come with a basic toolkit. For cars this usually includes a jack and wheel removal tools. Make sure that you know where to locate this.
- Make sure you know where the jacking points are that are used to lift the car safely.
- Make sure that you know the locations of the locking key if your wheels have locking nuts.

If you are riding a bicycle you should think about whether you need to carry a puncture repair kit and pump. Some people don't like carrying these things

because they are easily stolen. However, if you have a puncture when you are a few miles from home it can be very hard work getting back with a flat tyre.

It can be more complicated to remove a wheel or tyre from a scooter or motorcycle and, of course, it is very unusual for motorcycles to carry a spare. It is possible to buy special liquids which can be injected into a tyre, through the valve, to seal any puncture. In other cases you may have to call a breakdown organisation to come to your assistance.

Engine oil

- Check your oil level, using the dipstick, at least every fortnight and certainly before any long journey.
- A few cars have sealed engines and don't have a dipstick. These cars measure oil levels electronically and will either flash a warning light or use a recorded message to tell you if you need to put more oil in.
- Some cars also have 'long life' oil in them and this is changed when the car's computer tells you that it needs to be serviced. If you have this sort of car you must make sure that you only use the right sort of oil.
- Change the oil and filter at recommended service intervals.
- If you are using a lot of oil, it might indicate engine problems which should be investigated.

Water

- The coolant level should be checked regularly and topped up as necessary. To avoid injury, only attempt this when the engine is cold.
- Check the antifreeze concentration before winter.
- Antifreeze also prevents the build-up of corrosion within the cooling system and so should be checked on a regular basis.
- Not all scooters and motorcycles have a liquid cooling system. Some rely on the flow of air over the engine. You need to make sure you understand what sort you have because if it is liquid cooled and you forget to maintain it you could suddenly find the engine seizing up on you.

Power steering

The fluid reservoir for a power steering system needs to be checked regularly. However, it is not something that most people do. Generally you can rely on it being done when your car is serviced. If you feel your steering suddenly becoming heavy, or if a warning light shows on your dashboard, you should contact the garage where you have your servicing done.

Web wonders

Watch the following video clips:

http://www.youtube.com/
watch?v=1SP3ZVDeNYQ

http://www.youtube.com/
watch?v=4z7MrwVpirs

Wipers

Replace wipers at least once a year, as wiper blades wear down over time and smear the windscreen if they become worn.

Screenwash

It's a legal requirement that the screenwash system works, so top it up on a regular basis.

Windscreen

- Check the windscreen regularly for any chips or cracks as any damage may interfere with your vision or distract you attention. Some chips can be repaired – usually free of charge – depending on your insurance policy.
- Minor chips can grow and crack the glass so they should not be left unchecked.

Web wonders

Watch the following video clip:

http://www.youtube.com/
watch?v=yx71snsSAtE

Lights

- Check all lights weekly including indicators, brake lights and fog lights.
- Clean the lights regularly.
- In bad weather clean the lights during driving breaks.

Effective lights are particularly important if you are riding a scooter, motorcycle or bicycle. Not only do lights help you see where you are going but they also help other road users to see you. Most motorcycles are now fitted with lights which stay on all day. You must not turn these off. On a bicycle you must have a red light to the rear and a white light to the front. You can fit flashing lights and these can be very effective in making you visible to other road users.

Bodywork

- Any damage to the bodywork should be followed up quickly to prevent rust setting in.
- Many extended bodywork warranty schemes require annual inspection at the dealership – your vehicle manual will provide more information.

Exhaust

- If your exhaust is noisy, it may have a leak and this should be checked.
- The two emissions tested in the MOT are carbon monoxide (CO) and hydrocarbons (HC). If your car fails on either of these tests you will need to get the problem solved by an authorised service centre.

Here are some other simple tips:

- Check your belts, hoses and wiper blades every couple of months and replace them if there is any damage.
- On a scooter or motorcycle you should check the chain or drive belt and that the steering is moving freely.
- Check your battery for any loose or worn cabling or any corrosion on the battery terminals.

Remember: there is never a good time for a breakdown, and following these simple steps might save you a lot of money and hassle in the long term.

Mobile phones

Since December 2003, it has been illegal to use a hand-held mobile phone while driving. Breaking this law can lead to a £60 fine and three penalty points. It is possible that you could be prosecuted and taken to court, in which case fines will almost certainly be larger and disqualification is possible. The maximum fine in a court is £1000, or £2500 if the driver is driving a bus or a goods vehicle.

Where the use of a mobile phone has contributed to an accident, drivers can be prosecuted for careless driving, dangerous driving, or causing death by careless or dangerous driving. In such cases fines can be much higher, and prison is likely if a death is caused.

Remember that, although it is not illegal to use a hands-free phone, it is still a risky thing to do. It is always best to pull in somewhere safe if you need to have a conversation with somebody. It is never safe to send or receive text messages while you are on the move.

Did you know?

If you use a mobile phone while driving you are four times more likely to crash.

Reaction times for drivers using a phone are reduced by 50%.

Web wonders

Watch the following video clips:

http://www.youtube.com/watch?v=72gRlWXgD0o

http://www.youtube.com/watch?v=YNeicVxxDjQ

Think it through

Now take the driving test challenge!

http://think.direct.gov.uk/drivingchallenge/index.html

Explain the importance of co-operating and communicating with other road users

Explain how to communicate your intentions to other road users

When you are driving, you will not be the only road user; there will be others who will be observing you and responding to your actions and manoeuvres. For this reason there are rules of the road which are contained within the Highway Code. It is therefore important that you keep up to date with changes to the Highway Code. Ignorance is not an excuse for breaking the law.

One of the most important tools for communicating to other drivers is appropriate signalling and – in emergencies – using your horn. These are both important tools in communicating your intentions to other road users, so ensuring road safety.

Unfortunately not all drivers or riders are good at communicating their intentions. Times when this can cause particular problems are in overtaking or when negotiating a roundabout. This can cause confusion for other road users, not to mention the possibility of an accident. So it is important not simply to rely on the signals somebody gives. You also need to observe their speed and position on the road to be able to predict their next move with more certainty.

Here are some common-sense tips to follow:

1 Communicate your intentions to other road users using car lights, correct vehicle positioning and manual signals if needed.

2 Signal at the right time, the right place, and in time, and remember to cancel signals after you have made your move.

3 Position your vehicle appropriately to support the move that you intend to make.

4 Use the Mirrors Signal Manoeuvre (MSM) routine.

MSM is designed to avoid having accidents ourselves as well as helping us avoid causing accidents that will affect other road users. Before you make any vehicle manoeuvre, you need to use your mirrors to assess what is happening around you, then signal to show your intentions and then make your move, if safe to do so. This applies whether you are in a car, on a scooter or on a bicycle. You may not have mirrors on your bike but you can at least make sure you look around.

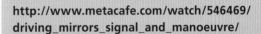

Web wonders

Watch the following video clip which shows the MSM manoeuvre:

http://www.metacafe.com/watch/546469/driving_mirrors_signal_and_manoeuvre/

Now watch the following video clip, which shows what could happen if MSM is not followed:

http://www.youtube.com/watch?v=IgOwDsF8ZFs

You should only use your horn when your vehicle is moving, and even then only in a real emergency to let other road users know your location. If you use it in the wrong way, at the wrong time, you may be committing an offence. Your horn is not a tool to let other road users know that you are annoyed with them!

Like the horn, flashing your headlights should only ever be used when there is a real emergency and you need to let other road users know of your location. It is also important to remember that somebody else flashing their lights at you, for example, at a junction does not mean that it is safe to proceed. The other driver may be doing their best to help you but you have to make your own decision. They may be wrong or you might have misunderstood what they were trying to tell you. Flashing your lights should not be used as a means of letting other road users know that you are annoyed with them.

There are also rules about the use of hazard warning lights. These should only be used when your vehicle is stopped and to warn other road users that you may be causing an obstruction. Hazard lights should not be used as a means of letting other road users know that you

- have parked your car for a short time to do an errand
- are being towed or are towing another vehicle, unless you are on a motorway or unrestricted dual carriageway.

You should cancel your hazard lights as soon as you are no longer causing an obstruction.

You should avoid displaying aggressive or violent behaviour to other road users – for example by shouting, **gesticulating** or tailgating. The chances are that this will just wind up other road users and make the situation worse. Keeping calm and polite and showing some courtesy might have a positive effect on other road users!

Explain how your behaviour might trigger negative behaviour in road users

Road rage

We all get stressed at times. There are times when we need to get somewhere quickly. If you are held up in traffic, or you think other people are driving slowly or badly, you may become stressed and show symptoms of 'road rage'.

Road rage can be as simple as shouting at other road users, or making inappropriate hand **gestures** to others. However, in some cases it can lead to much more dangerous situations involving serious attacks, fights and even death.

Road rage is an emotion that has recently developed due to our growing reliance on cars and other vehicles. We all make mistakes at times and just because a road user makes a dangerous manoeuvre, it does not mean that they are always a dangerous driver – they might just be having a bad day – as we all do. In these situations it is best to 'count to ten', take a deep breath and say to yourself, 'Well, at least that is over and done with.' Where a driver is making a series of dangerous manoeuvres, keep your distance, make a mental note of their number plate and call the police when safe to do so.

If you have carried out a manoeuvre that might have angered another person, try to show that you are sorry, if it is safe to do so: for example, by raising your hand to indicate 'Sorry, it was my fault.'

This should help to calm the situation. It is probably not a good idea to make eye contact with the other driver or try to communicate with them in any other way. Continue with your journey – safely.

Sadly, there have been some appalling examples of drivers taking out their road rage on riders, both of motorcycles and bicycles. If you are riding, it is particularly important to remember how vulnerable you are and how easily you could be seriously injured or killed in a confrontation with a driver of a car or truck.

If you feel intimidated by another road user, there are a few common-sense steps that you should take:

- Keep your car windows closed and door locked – particularly if you have to stop at traffic lights.
- Do not converse with the other driver.
- Do not respond to their gestures or speech.
- If you are worried, remember the registration number and call or visit the police.
- Do not go to your home address if the other person is following you – drive to a police station or other public place where you can get help.

Other simple tips include:

1 Don't drive too close to the car in front – this can be seen as intimidation as well as being a potential accident scenario. The Highway Code says that any car following another is responsible for stopping in time, so if you're driving too close to the car in front and they slam on their brakes and you run into them, it is your fault.

2 Remember that if somebody is stuck in a traffic jam it can be very frustrating for them to see a two-wheeled vehicle nipping down the gaps between the lanes. If you decide to do this, take particular care and acknowledge drivers who move out of the way for you.

3 Don't assume that all road rage incidents occur while you're on the road. Trying to locate a parking space can be stressful and there may be 'competition' to get a free space. Simple rules to follow include these:

- Avoid any situations that you feel might upset another driver – if you think the other person was there first, give up the space!
- Try to stay calm – getting stressed only makes the situation more difficult to handle.
- Think about the consequences before you enter a competition to find a free space!

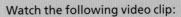

Think it through

Are you likely to suffer from road rage? Visit the following web link and take the road rage quiz.

http://www.quizplz.com/driving/road-rage-quiz.htm

Web wonders

Watch the following video clip:

http://www.youtube.com/watch?v=8SunrQam8aU&feature=related

Think it through

Follow the link below and read the article from the BBC news website, 'Road Rage Hits Most Drivers', published on Wednesday 13 August 2003, then answer the questions that follow.

http://news.bbc.co.uk/1/hi/uk/3146781.stm

1 How many drivers say that they have been the victim of road rage?

2 How many said that they have committed road rage?

3 Which part of the UK had the highest incidents of road rage?

4 What are the common characteristics of road rage that were displayed?

5 What are the factors associated with road rage?

Web wonders

Watch the following video clip. I wonder where these children picked up these attitudes? Their parents perhaps?

http://www.youtube.com/watch?v=2i8NUfl7tW4

End of book test

1 Before you make a U-turn in the road, you should

Select one answer

A give an arm signal as well as using your indicators

B look over your shoulder for a final check

C signal so that other drivers can slow down for you

D select a higher gear than normal.

2 You think the driver in the vehicle in front has forgotten to cancel their right indicator. You should

Select one answer

A flash your lights to alert the driver

B sound your horn before overtaking

C overtake on the left if there is room

D stay behind and not overtake.

3 A driver does something that upsets you. You should

Select one answer

A try not to react

B let them know how you feel

C flash your headlights several times

D sound your horn.

4 Before starting a journey it is wise to plan your route. How can you do this?

Select one answer

A Look at a map

B Look in your vehicle handbook

C Contact your local garage

D Check your vehicle registration document

5 The fluid level in your battery is low. What should you top it up with?

Select one answer

A Battery acid

B Distilled water

C Engine coolant

D Engine oil

6 You are driving along a country road. A horse and rider are approaching. What should you do?

Select two answers

A Increase your speed

B Sound your horn

C Drive slowly past

D Give plenty of room

E Flash your headlights

F Rev your engine

7 You stop for pedestrians waiting to cross at a zebra crossing. They do not start to cross. What should you do?

Select one answer

A Be patient and wait

B Carry on

C Wave them to cross

D Sound your horn

8 You are planning a long journey. Do you need to plan rest stops?

Select one answer

A Yes, regular stops help concentration

B No, you will be less tired if you get there as soon as possible

C Yes, you should plan to stop every half hour

D No, only fuel stops will be needed

9 You are following a slow-moving vehicle on a narrow country road. There is a junction just ahead on the right. What should you do?

Select one answer

A Stay behind until you are past the junction

B Overtake after checking your mirrors and signalling

C Accelerate quickly to pass before the junction

D Slow down and prepare to overtake on the left

10 'Tailgating' means

Select one answer

A using the rear door of a hatchback car

B following another vehicle too closely

C driving with rear fog lights on

D reversing into a parking space

11 Road humps, chicanes, and road narrowings are

Select one answer

A used to increase traffic speed

B always at major roadworks

C at toll-bridge approaches only

D traffic calming measures.

12 You are following a vehicle on a wet road. You should leave a time gap of at least

Select one answer

A one second

B two seconds

C three seconds

D four seconds

13 Which two are badly affected if the tyres are under-inflated?

Select two answers

A Braking

B Steering

C Changing gear

D Parking

14 At which type of crossing are cyclists allowed to ride across with pedestrians?

Select one answer

A Pelican

B Puffin

C Toucan

D Zebra

15 You are approaching two cyclists. They approach a roundabout in the left-hand lane. In which direction should you expect the cyclists to go?

Select one answer

A Right

B Any direction

C Left

D Straight ahead

16 What is the most likely cause of high fuel consumption?

Select one answer

A Poor steering control

B Accelerating around bends

C Harsh braking and accelerating

D Staying in high gears

17 Your mobile phone rings while you are travelling. You should

Select one answer

A pull up in a suitable place

B stop immediately

C answer it immediately

D pull up at the nearest kerb

18 Why should you always reduce your speed when travelling in fog?

Select one answer

A The engine will take longer to warm up

B The brakes do not work as well

C It is more difficult to see events ahead

D You will be dazzled by oncoming headlights

19 At a pelican crossing, the flashing amber light means you must

Select one answer

- A   stop and wait for the green light
- B   stop and wait for the red light
- C   give way to pedestrians waiting to cross
- D   give way to pedestrians already on the crossing

20 You are at the scene of an accident. Someone is suffering from shock. You should

Select four answers

- A   keep them warm
- B   reassure then constantly
- C   offer them a cigarette
- D   avoid leaving them alone
- E   give them a warm drink
- F   avoid moving them if possible

21 Which of the following may cause loss of concentration?

Select four answers

- A   Loud music
- B   Arguing with a passenger
- C   Using a mobile phone
- D   Putting on a CD
- E   Stopping regularly to rest
- F   Pulling up to tune the radio

22 What is the braking distance when travelling at 30 m.p.h.?

- A   14 metres
- B   19 metres
- C   25 metres
- D   30 metres

23 A cover note is a document issued before you receive your

Select one answer

- A   driving licence
- B   insurance certificate
- C   registration document
- D   MOT certificate

24 A newly qualified driver must

Select one answer

- A   display green L plates
- B   not exceed 40 m.p.h. for twelve months
- C   be accompanied on a motorway
- D   have valid motor insurance

25 Which **three** of these do you need before you can drive legally?

Select three answers

- A   A valid driving licence
- B   A valid tax disc displayed on your vehicle
- C   A vehicle service record
- D   Proper insurance cover
- E   Breakdown cover
- F   A vehicle handbook

26 You are driving on a clear night. There is a steady stream of oncoming traffic. The national speed limit applies. Which lights should you use?

Select one answer

- A   Full beam headlights
- B   Sidelights
- C   Dipped headlights
- D   Fog lights

27 What style of driving causes increased risk to everyone?

Select one answer

A Considerate

B Defensive

C Competitive

D Responsible

28 You are approaching a red light at a puffin crossing. Pedestrians are on the crossing. The red light will stay on until

Select one answer

A you start to edge forward onto the crossing

B the pedestrians have reached a safe position

C the pedestrians are clear of the front of your vehicle

D a driver from the opposite direction reaches the crossing

29 You should **only** flash your headlights to other road users

Select one answer

A to show that you are giving way

B to show you are about to turn

C to tell them that you have right of way

D to let them know that you are there.

30 What should you use your horn for?

Select one answer

A To alert others to your presence

B To allow you the right of way

C To greet other road users

D To signal your annoyance

31 On a long motorway journey boredom can cause you to feel sleepy. You should

Select two answers

A leave the motorway and find a safe place to stop

B keep looking around at the surrounding landscape

C drive faster to complete your journey sooner

D ensure a supply of fresh air into your vehicle

E stop on the hard shoulder for a rest

32 Which **four** are most likely to cause you to lose concentration while you are driving?

Select four answers

A Using a mobile phone

B Talking into a microphone

C Tuning your car radio

D Looking at a map

E Checking the mirrors

F Using the demisters

33 It is a very windy day and you are about to overtake a cyclist. What should you do?

Select one answer

A Overtake very closely

B Keep close as you pass

C Sound your horn repeatedly

D Allow extra room

34 You must stop when signalled to do so by which **three** of these?

Select three answers

A A police officer

B A pedestrian

C A school crossing patrol

D A bus driver

E A red traffic light

35 As well as planning your route before starting a journey, you should also plan an alternative route. Why is this?

Select one answer

A To let another driver overtake

B Your first route may be blocked

C To avoid a railway level crossing

D In case you have to avoid emergency vehicles

36 You are carrying two thirteen-year-old children and their parents in your car. Who is responsible for seeing that the children wear seatbelts?

Select one answer

A The children's parents

B You, the driver

C The front-seat passenger

D The children

37 What should you do when leaving your vehicle?

Select one answer

A Put valuable documents under seats

B Remove all valuables

C Cover valuables with a blanket

D Leave the interior light on

38 You break down on a motorway. You need to call for help. Why may it be better to use an emergency roadside telephone rather than a mobile phone?

Select one answer

A It connects you to a local garage

B Using a mobile phone will distract other drivers

C It allows easy location by the emergency services

D Mobile phones do not work on motorways

39 You are allowed to stop on a motorway when you

Select one answer

A need to walk and get fresh air

B wish to pick up hitchhikers

C are told to do so by flashing red lights

D need to use a mobile phone

40 You are on a motorway. A large box falls onto the road from a lorry. The lorry does not stop. You should

Select one answer

A go to the next emergency telephone and report the hazard

B catch up with the lorry and try to get the driver's attention

C stop close to the box until the police arrive

D pull over to the hard shoulder, then remove the box.

Answers to tasks and questions

Introduction
Statistics
153,937 road casualties

Unit 1
Task 1: Prepare for a journey by road
Identify the modes of transport you could use for a journey
Page 2: Three modes of transport

(Note: this list is not exhaustive.)

1. Air – aeroplane, helicopter, hot-air balloon, para-glider, glider.

2. Rail – tram, passenger train, haulage/goods train, monorail.

3. Sea – ferry, barge, cruise ship, yacht, canoe, hovercraft.

Outline which is the most appropriate mode of transport in your circumstances
Page 3: Safety

1. Safest mode of transport: air; least safe: motorcycle.

2. Bus

3. Water

4. Foot

5. Motorcycle is the least safest mode of transport for all criteria – distance, number of journeys and time.

6. Bus and rail are safest, as they both appear more as first or second in all three columns.

Eco-driving
Page 5: Electric cars

Although electric cars are often in the news, they have been around for a number of years. As a result of increases in fuel costs, they are now becoming more popular. Electric cars are powered by an electric motor which takes its power from battery packs positioned within the car. The batteries tend to be either nickel–metal hydride or lithium-ion and are usually charged from a mains power supply. It can take up to twelve hours for a full charge. Some electric cars have a system that tops up the power supply from the movement of the brakes.

Current electric vehicles in the UK tend to be smaller but three-seaters are now available. They are able to achieve a range of 40 to 100 miles, with top speeds from 25 to 45 m.p.h. For this reason they are commonly used by city drivers, where distance or speed is not an issue.

Because electric cars have no emissions, they generally have many tax advantages.

Hybrid cars

Hybrid cars generally use a combination of two power sources, the most common hybrids being electric and petrol-driven.

The battery is charged as the car moves and powers the electric motor. This usually copes with low speeds such as in city driving. The petrol engine kicks in when faster speeds or more distance is needed.

The petrol engine recharges the battery cells (as does braking), and so hybrid cars do not need to be plugged into an external power supply. This combination of battery power and internal combustion engine produces less pollution and CO_2 as no gases are released when the electric motor is running.

Cars using LPG

Liquefied Petroleum Gas (LPG) is a natural hydrocarbon fuel made up of propane and butane. LPG is better for the environment as it produces far less CO_2 than petrol, and fewer particulates and nitrogen oxides than diesel. LPG can be used in petrol-driven cars, which can be converted at a cost of around £1500 to £2000. Conversion includes the installation of a second fuel tank for the LPG, which means the vehicle can switch between petrol and LPG.

LPG is recognised as a major energy source and currently offered by about 10% of refuelling stations.

Think of a number

The company would save £37.50 per week.

Plan the best route for your journey

Page 6: Day trip planner to Falkirk and Edinburgh

A sample planner is provided below. This may not be the same as yours due to transport timetable changes.

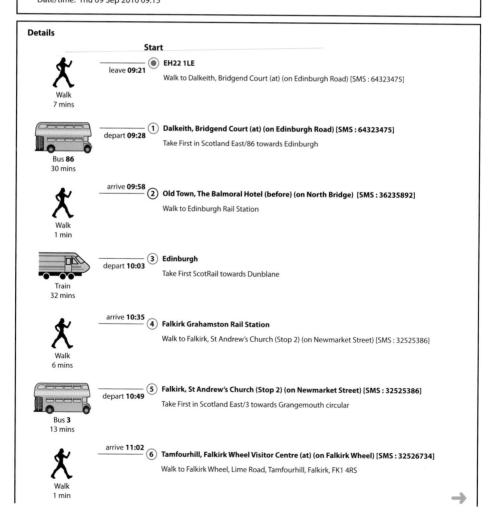

Requested journey
From: EH22 1LE
First location: Falkirk Wheel, Lime Road, Tamfourhill, Falkirk, FK1 4RS
Second location: Edinburgh Castle (Historic Scotland), Edinburgh Castle, Castle Hill, Edinburgh, EH1 2NG
Date/time: Thu 09 Sep 2010 09:15

Length of 2 hour stay: (s)
Length of 2 hour stay: (s)
Return to start: Yes

Details

Start

Walk
7 mins
leave **09:21**   ◉ **EH22 1LE**
Walk to Dalkeith, Bridgend Court (at) (on Edinburgh Road) [SMS : 64323475]

Bus **86**
30 mins
depart **09:28**   ① **Dalkeith, Bridgend Court (at) (on Edinburgh Road) [SMS : 64323475]**
Take First in Scotland East/86 towards Edinburgh

Walk
1 min
arrive **09:58**   ② **Old Town, The Balmoral Hotel (before) (on North Bridge) [SMS : 36235892]**
Walk to Edinburgh Rail Station

Train
32 mins
depart **10:03**   ③ **Edinburgh**
Take First ScotRail towards Dunblane

Walk
6 mins
arrive **10:35**   ④ **Falkirk Grahamston Rail Station**
Walk to Falkirk, St Andrew's Church (Stop 2) (on Newmarket Street) [SMS : 32525386]

Bus **3**
13 mins
depart **10:49**   ⑤ **Falkirk, St Andrew's Church (Stop 2) (on Newmarket Street) [SMS : 32525386]**
Take First in Scotland East/3 towards Grangemouth circular

Walk
1 min
arrive **11:02**   ⑥ **Tamfourhill, Falkirk Wheel Visitor Centre (at) (on Falkirk Wheel) [SMS : 32526734]**
Walk to Falkirk Wheel, Lime Road, Tamfourhill, Falkirk, FK1 4RS

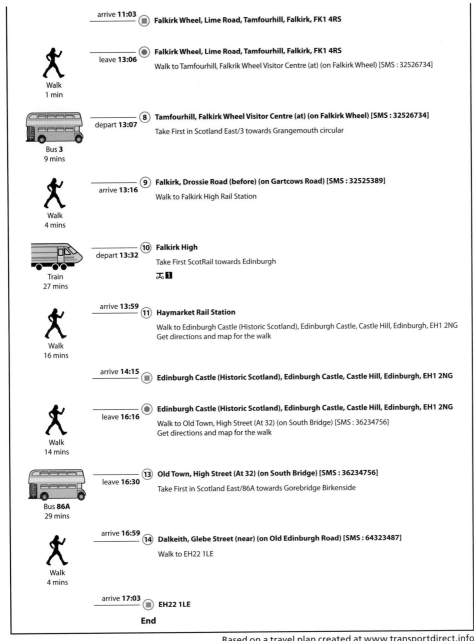

arrive **11:03** Falkirk Wheel, Lime Road, Tamfourhill, Falkirk, FK1 4RS

Walk
1 min
leave **13:06** Falkirk Wheel, Lime Road, Tamfourhill, Falkirk, FK1 4RS
Walk to Tamfourhill, Falkrik Wheel Visitor Centre (at) (on Falkirk Wheel) [SMS : 32526734]

Bus 3
9 mins
depart **13:07** (8) Tamfourhill, Falkirk Wheel Visitor Centre (at) (on Falkirk Wheel) [SMS : 32526734]
Take First in Scotland East/3 towards Grangemouth circular

Walk
4 mins
arrive **13:16** (9) Falkirk, Drossie Road (before) (on Gartcows Road) [SMS : 32525389]
Walk to Falkirk High Rail Station

Train
27 mins
depart **13:32** (10) Falkirk High
Take First ScotRail towards Edinburgh

Walk
16 mins
arrive **13:59** (11) Haymarket Rail Station
Walk to Edinburgh Castle (Historic Scotland), Edinburgh Castle, Castle Hill, Edinburgh, EH1 2NG
Get directions and map for the walk

arrive **14:15** Edinburgh Castle (Historic Scotland), Edinburgh Castle, Castle Hill, Edinburgh, EH1 2NG

Walk
14 mins
leave **16:16** Edinburgh Castle (Historic Scotland), Edinburgh Castle, Castle Hill, Edinburgh, EH1 2NG
Walk to Old Town, High Street (At 32) (on South Bridge) [SMS : 36234756]
Get directions and map for the walk

Bus 86A
29 mins
leave **16:30** (13) Old Town, High Street (At 32) (on South Bridge) [SMS : 36234756]
Take First in Scotland East/86A towards Gorebridge Birkenside

Walk
4 mins
arrive **16:59** (14) Dalkeith, Glebe Street (near) (on Old Edinburgh Road) [SMS : 64323487]
Walk to EH22 1LE

arrive **17:03** EH22 1LE

End

Based on a travel plan created at www.transportdirect.info

Outline how you would decide if you and/or your companions are fit to travel

Page 8: Legal drugs

Side effects of antihistamines:

- drowsiness/sleepiness
- sore head
- blurred vision
- constipation
- dry mouth
- dizziness
- difficulty urinating
- confusion.

Page 9: Illegal drugs

Cocaine

A drug that acts as a stimulant and can affect your ability to judge both speed and distance, particularly stopping distances. It affects your sense of light and sound and can make you feel over-confident in your own abilities, which can make your driving erratic, unpredictable and dangerous. Although it is a stimulant that can initially make you feel alert, eventually it can make you feel tired and drowsy, and so there is a danger that you could fall asleep when driving.

LSD

LSD can make you hallucinate and see things that are not there, which can be very dangerous if driving a vehicle. It can also heighten your sensitivity to light and sound and so cause distraction from driving. It is likely to affect your co-ordination and reaction times.

Heroin

Heroin affects your co-ordination and sense of reality as well as causing tiredness, nausea and breathing problems, all of which can impact on road safety.

Ecstasy

A drug that acts as a stimulant but which also makes you hallucinate (makes you see things that are not there). Ecstasy can affect your sense of vision and sound and so affect your driving ability. It can make you become over-confident and more likely to take dangerous risks.

Speed

Speed can make you feel very alert and over-confident, which can be highly dangerous for driving. It can distort your thinking and make you feel anxious and prone to panic attacks, and lose co-ordination.

Page 10: Alcohol

The 'totting up' system

The number of penalty points varies according to the seriousness of the motoring offence, with more serious driving offences attracting the highest number of points.

- Minor offences carry the minimum number – 2 points.
- Common offences such as speeding in a 30 m.p.h. area, or using a mobile phone when driving – 3 points.

The court can determine other penalty points to be issued to a person, depending on the severity of the offence. If you get a total of 12 or more penalty points over a period of three years, you will usually lose your licence.

TT99

This means that you have reached the limit of 12 penalty points in three years, and you are likely to lose your licence – meaning you will be disqualified from driving.

New Drivers Act

Under the New Drivers Act your driving licence will be cancelled if you get a total of 6 or more penalty points within two years of passing your first driving test.

Page 10: Tiredness/fatigue

Signs of tiredness in the video clip: yawning, loss of concentration, rubbing eyes, blinking, tiredness, sleeping.

Page 11: Emotional well-being

Happiness: state of being positive and generally feeling good about oneself and others. This might have a positive effect on driving as you'll probably be less stressed.

Fear: state of being worried about something or nervous that something bad might happen. This might lead to being over-cautious: for example, driving at a slower speed than necessary, or hesitating and causing confusion for other road users.

Anger: state of being annoyed or cross with someone or something. This might lead to less cautious driving or more aggressive driving, taking more risks, and being less patient.

Aggressiveness: state of wanting to behave in a negative manner towards people. This might encourage risk-taking and make other drivers feel threatened, for example by road rage.

Page 11: Physical health

Diabetes and epilepsy

Diabetes: you might suffer a diabetic 'low' and so be less in control of your vehicle.

Epilepsy: you might have a seizure or fit and as a result be unable to control your vehicle.

Task 1: End of Task test

1 B, 2 A, 3 C, 4 A, 5 C, 6 A, 7 B, 8 C, 9 B, 10 A

Task 2: Identify what needs to be considered before going on a journey by road

State the documentation required for using a vehicle on the road

Page 16: Driving licence

DVLA: The Driver and Vehicle Licensing Agency assists with road safety and general law enforcement by maintaining registers of drivers and vehicles and collecting vehicle excise duty (car tax).

Based in Swansea, in South Wales, the DVLA was originally known as the Driver and Vehicle Licensing Centre or DVLC. It has a network of offices throughout the UK. There are several responsibilities of the DVLA, including the following:

- the issuing of driving licences and DVLA registrations
- organising the collection of excise duties on vehicles (also referred to as road fund licence or road tax)
- selling private number plates.

You can pay your car tax online, by telephone, or through the Post Office.

Page 18: MOT certificate

The cost of an MOT certificate (December 2011): motorcycle £29.65; car £54.85.

Page 19: Vehicle excise duty

Cost of VED (December 2011): Band A car £0

Band H car £190 (1 year) / £104.50 (6 months)

Band M car £460 (1 year) / £253 (6 months)

Motorcycle over 600 cc £74 (1 year) / £40.70 (6 months)

Motor insurance

Page 20: The cost of motor insurance

Factors affecting the cost of insurance

Description of factor	Increase insurance cost	Decrease insurance cost
An experienced driver of 15 years with no accidents and no penalty points on his licence		✓
A new male driver aged 19	✓	
A new male driver aged 35		✓
A car with built-in car alarm and engine immobiliser		✓
Driver of a Porsche car	✓	
Owner of a 5-year-old 1-litre Fiat Punto		✓
Car which is parked in a secure garage overnight		✓
Third party only insurance cover		✓
Car which is parked on the street in the city centre at night	✓	

Page 21: Insurance terms

Policy excess is the amount you have to pay if you make a claim on your insurance. For example, an excess of £50 means that you must pay the first £50 of any claim yourself. Policies with an excess are generally a bit cheaper than those without.

A **cover note** is a temporary certificate of insurance that allows you to drive on the road straight away, when you have bought car insurance and while you are waiting for the insurance company to issue the documents and post them out to you.

Renewal notice: A car insurance policy usually runs for twelve months. When your policy is about to come to an end, the insurance company will send you a renewal notice, usually at least 21 days before the current insurance policy expires, inviting you to renew your insurance with them. The renewal notice will contain details of the new policy on offer, including the premium and any changes to the cover or service.

A **policy document** is a contract of insurance, describing the term, coverage and premiums. It is also sometime just called the policy.

The **premium** is the amount paid for the purchase of insurance.

The driving test

Page 24: Email to Emma

The cost of a car driving test is £31 for the theory test and £62 for the practical test (or £75 if at the weekend or in the evening). (Correct at December 2011.)

Page 24: Email to Rav

The cost of a motorcycle driving test is £31 for the theory test; £15.50 for module one; £75 for module two (or £88.50 if at the weekend or in the evening). (Correct at December 2011.)

Note: Answers are not supplied to the other parts of this Write it down activity.

Task 2: End of Task test

1 B, C, E; 2 A, B; 3 A, B, E; 4 B; 5 B; 6 A, D; 7 C; 8 B; 9 B; 10 B, C

Task 3: Understand the road and use it safely

Identify road types, junctions and pedestrian crossings and describe their functions

Road types

Page 29: Leeds road map

1   A58(M)/A64(M) and M621

2   A647

3   It is orange in colour on the map

4   B6159 / Harehills Lane

Road junctions

Page 30: Web clips

Message: Look out for motorcyclists when driving on the road.

Page 31: Lorry driver

The lorry driver is making an incorrect movement because he is trying to turn right across a busy dual carriageway by blocking traffic on the left-hand carriageway.

Identify traffic signals, road signs and markings

Page 34: Traffic signals

1 C, 2 D, 3 A, 4 B, 5 G, 6 E, 7 F

Page 35: Motorway signals

A   You must not proceed further in this lane.

B   The left-hand lane ahead is closed.

C   Accident ahead and speed limit temporarily reduced to 30 m.p.h.

Page 35: Other traffic signals

Cyclists

1   Left hand extended to left.

2   Left hand raised or right hand extended to right.

Left Turn

Right Turn

Page 36: Signals by authorised officials

A   Traffic approaching from front to stop

B   Traffic approaching from both front and behind to stop

C   Traffic approaching from behind to stop

D   Traffic approaching from side to progress

E   Traffic approaching from front to progress

F   Traffic approaching from behind to progress

G   All vehicles must stop

H   Not ready to cross pedestrians

I   Barrier to stop pedestrians crossing

J   Ready to cross pedestrians – vehicles must stop

Page 37: Order signs

A   20 m.p.h. speed limit

B   30 m.p.h. speed limit (following the ending of a 20 m.p.h. speed limit)

C   School crossing patrol

D   Maximum speed 40 m.p.h.

E   National speed limit applies

F   Stop and give way

G   Give way to traffic on major road

H   No vehicles except bicycles being pushed

I   No entry for vehicles

J   No right turn

K   No left turn

L   No U turns

M   Give priority to vehicles from opposite direction

N   No overtaking

O   No motor vehicles

P   Manually operated Stop sign

Q   Manually operated Go sign

R   No buses

S   No cycling

T   No towed caravans

U   No vehicles carrying explosives

V   No vehicles over the length shown

W   No vehicles over the height shown

X   No vehicles over the width shown

Y   No vehicles on bridge that are over the weight limit shown

Z   No good vehicles over the weight shown unless loading/unloading

AA   No waiting

BB   No stopping

CC   No stopping during the times shown

DD   Parking restricted to permit holders

Page 39: Warning signs

A 34, B 7, C 5, D 24, E 30, F 29, G 6, H 17, I 8, J 4, K 25, L 36, M 3, N 2, O 9, P 27, Q 32, R 12, S 13, T 37, U 16, V 14, W 15, X 41, Y 21, Z 44, AA 22, BB 42, CC 39, DD 33, EE 28, FF 11, GG 1, HH 18, II 19, JJ 40, KK 20, LL 23, MM 26, NN 31, OO 35, PP 38, QQ 45, RR 10, SS 43

Page 42: Directional signs

Sign 1 – half a mile to Junction 4 leading to A404 Marlow. Outer two lanes for Birmingham and Oxford on M40.

Sign 2 – half a mile to Junction 2 leading to A46 (M69) Leicester and Coventry (E). Straight ahead for M6 to the North West, Birmingham and Coventry (N).

Page 42: South Offen (B4113) straight ahead. There is a ring road to both left and right at the junction ahead. The junction ahead on the left leads to Darsley on the A411, and to the train station and free parking. The junction ahead on the right leads to Haven Bridge on the A411 and the Roman villa tourist attraction.

Page 47: Waiting and loading restrictions

A   No waiting at any time

B   Waiting is limited to the duration specified in the sign

C   No loading or unloading at the times shown

D   No waiting during the times shown

E   Loading bay

F   No loading or unloading at any time

G   Keep entrance clear of stationary vehicles at all times

H   Warning of Give Way ahead

I   Bus stop only

J   Lane for bus use only

K   Box junction

L   Do not block this part of the road

State the factors that affect a safe road speed

Page 48: Speed limits

Road sign indicating 60 m.p.h. speed limit.

Identify how different road users are affected by stopping distances

Page 50: Stopping distances

A   36

B   72

C   120

Page 50: Factors affecting stopping distance

1   Weather conditions can reduce visibility: for example darkness, fog, snow and rain will increase stopping distance.

2   Wet roads will increase stopping distance as there will be less contact between the tyre and the road surface.

3   Older vehicles may require a longer stopping distance unless regularly maintained.

4   Using a hand-held mobile phone while driving is an offence. Even using a hands-free mobile will increase your stopping distance, as your concentration will be divided between using the phone and driving.

Identify how and where to leave a vehicle safely and securely

Page 51: Anti-theft devices

The following answers are illustrative only.

Alarm services

A car alarm is usually an electronic device installed in a vehicle to discourage theft of the vehicle and of its contents. The alarm works by providing a high-volume sound, such as a siren, when someone tampers with your car. Alarms can also work by flashing some of the vehicle's lights, and interrupting various electrical circuits necessary for the car to start.

Remote keyless entry systems

A remote keyless system is one designed to allow or deny access to vehicles – you gain access to the vehicle without the need for a physical key.

Steering wheel locks

The steering lock is a brightly coloured lock that restricts the removal or movement of the steering wheel and airbag and so makes it difficult for a thief to drive the vehicle away.

Tracking devices

These are electronic gadgets attached to a cars which allow the movement of the car to be tracked by a another person. If the car is stolen, it can be traced or tracked by this device.

VIN etching

VIN etching is a measure to reduce motor vehicle theft. It usually involves the use of a stencil and glass etching paste to mark a vehicle identification number (VIN) onto the windshield and windows. Thieves would need to replace the glass before selling the stolen vehicle.

Immobilisers

An immobiliser is a piece of electronic theft prevention equipment that is wired into your car's engine and ignition system. When the immobiliser is active, you can't start the engine, even with the key.

Task 3: End of Task test A

1 A, 2 B, 3 B, 4 A, 5 C

End of Task test B

1 B, 2 B, 3 A, 4 D, 5 C

Task 4: Describe how to use the roads with regards to the Highway Code and other road users

Describe what to do if you are in a vehicle that breaks down

Page 56: Breaking down on the motorway or dual carriageway

A   In case the car is hit from behind by another vehicle, having its wheels turned to the left will stop the car being moved onto the main carriageway.

B   Stop near the phone to minimise the amount of time you will be walking at the side of the carriageway.

C   Switch on the lights to ensure that your vehicle is visible.

D   Leave by the left-hand door so that you do not step onto the carriageway where there is moving traffic.

E   Wait on the far side to ensure that you are well away from traffic travelling on the carriageway.

Page 58: Describe what to do if you are involved in, or are a witness to, an incident

What should I do?

If there is damage to someone else's vehicle or property, you should exchange the following with the owner of the other vehicle:

* registration numbers
* names and addresses
* details of the owner if not yourself.

If you exchange details, you are not obliged to report the incident to the police as long as no one is injured.

If the collision does result in injury to any passenger, you must also give insurance details and report it to the police within 24 hours.

What happens when I report the collision?

You will need to speak to a police officer. This may involve waiting for someone to become available.

You will need to provide your driving licence, insurance details and MOT certificate. If you fail to do so within a practical time period you can be prosecuted.

Do I have to make a statement?

At the police station you may be required to give your version of events in a statement. This does not necessarily mean you will have to be a witness in criminal proceedings. If that is required, a Witness Citation will be issued as written confirmation.

What do I do if the other driver wasn't insured?

Compensation for injuries received in a road accident usually depends on insurance.

If the other party is not insured, you may be able to claim compensation from the Motor Insurers' Bureau. They take into account claims for personal injury caused by uninsured and untraced drivers.

Be aware that you can only claim once for the same accident. You cannot claim on your own insurance and against another driver.

Answers to page 58 are adapted from www.safermotoring.co.uk.

If a stolen vehicle is insured by the real owner, personal injury and damage to property claims must be handled by the real owner's insurance company.

Should I contact my insurance company?

Most insurance companies request that you inform them about accidents even if a claim is not being made. You will be sent a motor accident report form to complete.

Can I get the other driver's details from the police?

Under the Data Protection Act, the police are limited in the information about road accidents that they can give out.

If your road accident is being investigated, you can request the following:

- the accident file computer reference number
- the identification number of the reporting officer
- the station at which the reporting officer is based.

These details will let your insurance company get information about the incident from the police.

Will I be prosecuted?

Not necessarily. To be brought before the court there needs to be a clear indication of careless driving or driving without due care and attention.

My car is damaged. What happens next?

For road safety reasons, a damaged vehicle must be taken away as soon as possible. The police may organise a contractor to remove the vehicle. You are accountable for any charges. You can choose the garage to call out if they can meet the call-out time.

Task 4: End of Task test

1 D; 2 A, B, C; 3 B, E; 4 D; 5 B, E; 6 B; 7 C; 8 D

Unit 2

Task 1: Explain how attitudes of yourself and others can affect safe road use

Identify own relevant characteristics

Page 62: Positive and negative characteristics

Positive characteristics	Negative characteristics
caring	uncaring, unfeeling
cheerful	cheerless, gloomy, grumpy
courteous	rude, impolite
perseveres, endures	relents, gives up
friendly	unfriendly, distant, aloof, hostile
positive	negative
responsive	unresponsive, unreceptive
self-confident	unconfident, insecure
sensitive	insensitive, indifferent
thoughtful towards others	thoughtless, inconsiderate, callous

Task 2: Identify key factors to consider before setting out on a road journey

Identify the risks and responsibilities of carrying passengers, animals and goods

Seatbelts

Page 65: Crash simulator

No seatbelts:

- Adult male dies.
- Adult female survives but has difficulty walking.
- Child dies.

With seatbelts:

- Adult male survives but with some injury.
- Adult female has minor injuries.
- Child survives with minor injuries.

The main difference is that they all survive.

No seatbelts – 20 m.p.h.:

- Adult male survives but with major injuries.
- Adult female survives but takes a long time to recover.
- Child survives.

The main difference is that they survive but the adults are badly injured.

Page 66: Seatbelt laws

1 The person occupying the seat.

2 Because of the risk of crushing or suffocation if the airbag is inflated.

3 The driver of the vehicle.

4 Above this height, a person can wear a seatbelt. Below this height a person has to wear a child restraint.

5 £60 fixed penalty fine or £500 fine if it goes to court.

Page 67: The risk associated with carrying passengers

1 The passenger feeling ill and being sick: stop the car until the passenger feels better, or drop person off at their house if it is not too far away.

2 The passenger being boisterous and singing loudly: tell then to quieten down. If they don't, stop in a safe place until they do.

3 The passenger turning up the radio too loud: tell them not to or switch the radio off.

4 The passenger interfering with the driving process: stop the car somewhere safe and tell them not to continue with this behaviour.

Identify the legal requirements for travelling using a vehicle

Breaking the law and penalties

Page 69: Penalties

1 Two years

2 £60

3 3 points

4 £2500

5 £5000 fine, £200 fixed penalty fine, 6–8 penalty points, 6 points if fixed penalty; discretionary prison sentence.

Task 3: Explain the importance of co-operating and communicating with other road users

Explain how your behaviour might trigger negative behaviour in road users

Page 75: Road rage

1 20 per cent

2 70% of those questioned

3 South of England

4 Gesticulating, physical and verbal abuse

5 Congestion, stress

End of book test

1 B; 2 D; 3 A; 4 A; 5 B; 6 C, D; 7 A; 8 A; 9 A; 10 B; 11 D; 12 B; 13 A, B; 14 C; 15 B; 16 C; 17 A; 18 C; 19 D; 20 A, B, D, F; 21 A, B, C, D; 22 A; 23 B; 24 D; 25 A, B, D; 26 C; 27 C; 28 B; 29 D; 30 A; 31 A, D; 32 A, B, C, D; 33 D; 34 A, C, E; 35 B; 36 B; 37 B; 38 C; 39 C; 40 A

Glossary

AA Automobile Association, a motoring organisation

antihistamines medicine used to treat allergies or colds

anxious feeling stressed or worried

arbitrary unreasonable

attitude a way of regarding or thinking about a person or thing, especially when it affects behaviour

BAC blood–alcohol concentration, a measure of alcohol in the blood

BS Kitemark British standard safety symbol often displayed on items

carriageway a road used by vehicles; a dual carriageway usually has two lanes for traffic in each direction, often separated by a barrier

casualty someone killed or injured in an accident

CCTV Closed Circuit Television, cameras used to monitor people or places

claim a demand for compensation under an insurance policy, for example for an accident; to make such a demand

community service a sentence which requires the criminal to work for the good of the community

companion a person travelling with you

cycling proficiency test a test designed to assess the competence of a cyclist

debris rubble or rubbish

destination the end point aimed at in a journey

deterrent something that stops or discourages someone from doing something

diabetes an illness in which the body does not produce enough insulin, which if not controlled well can lead to convulsions and loss of consciousness

disqualification having your driving licence taken from you

distraction something that affects your ability to concentrate

drowsiness feeling tired and sleepy

DVLA Driver and Vehicle Licensing Agency, responsible for driving licences, car registration and vehicle tax

E mark European standard safety symbol often displayed on items

eco-safe a way of driving with the environment in mind

emissions gases produced by vehicles

endorsement a record of details of a driving offence on a driving licence

enforce to make sure that a law or rule is obeyed

environment the surroundings in which we live

epilepsy an illness that can affect the signals in the brain and cause seizures and loss of consciousness

erratic strange or unpredictable

eye-witness someone who has observed something that happened

fatality death or an accident resulting in death

fatigue extreme tiredness

feedback information or a report back about a piece of work

fluorescent very bright, light-reflecting

gesticulating making hand movements, especially rude or threatening ones

gesture a body movement that indicates something to someone about how you feel

goods possessions, especially things bought or sold

GPS Global Positioning System

greenhouse gas a gas such as CO_2 that contributes to the 'greenhouse effect', the warming of the atmosphere when the sun's heat cannot escape

grounding the underside of a vehicle touching or getting stuck on the road surface

hard shoulder the strip of road surface running along the edge of a motorway

hazard a danger

Highway Code the rules of the road

hydraulic operated or moved by the effect of liquid being forced through a pipe or tube

ignition the device that starts the car by turning a key in the switch

influence to affect something or make it likely to happen

intentions what someone is planning to do

junction a place where two or more roads meet or join

legislation an item of law

LGV a large goods vehicle, such as a lorry

maintenance keeping something in good condition

manoeuvre a movement or series of movements carried out in a vehicle, such as turning or reversing

medication pills or tablets used to treat an illness

minimise to reduce something to its least possible extent or impact

mode a way of doing something; a mode of transport is a type or means of moving or travelling

moped a motorcycle of low power, under 50 cc

MOT Ministry of Transport; usually refers to the compulsory test to ensure a vehicle is roadworthy

obligatory something that must be done, enforced by law

oblige to require someone to do something

offence breaking the law

passenger someone (other than the driver) travelling in a vehicle

PCV Passenger Carrying Vehicle, for example a bus

pedestrian a person who is travelling on foot

penalty a punishment for breaking the law

penalty points points added to a driver's licence that can lead to disqualification

peripheral (i.e. vision) the extreme edges of your vision ('out of the corner of your eye')

pillion passenger a person carried as a passenger on a motorcycle

premium the amount you have to pay an insurance company to provide insurance

provisional licence the initial licence issued to a learner before passing the full driving test

quotation a statement of the expected cost of something, for example a car repair or an insurance premium

RAC a motoring organisation, formerly known as the Royal Automobile Club

reaction the particular way you act as a result of something else that has happened

regulations rules and laws

responsible accountable for what you do or say; reliable and sensible

restraint a device used to hold something in place

restriction a regulation to prevent you from doing something

road network the road system and how it connects together

r.p.m. revolutions per minute, a measure of the frequency with which the main drive shaft of an engine revolves

satnav Satellite Navigation System, a device used to help plan journeys

scenario a potential event or circumstance

SORN Statutory Off Road Notification, a certificate to state that a car is not being used on the road for a period of time

statistics information about a subject in terms of numbers

stringent strict

temporary for a limited time, not permanent

urban in the city

VED Vehicle Excise Duty, car or vehicle tax

visibility the ability to be seen

VOSA Vehicle and Operator Services Agency, the organisation that administers MOT certification and some types of vehicle licensing

vulnerable capable of being wounded or hurt

warranty a written guarantee that something you have bought will be repaired if it breaks down

witness to see or hear something happening; a person who has seen an incident and can testify to that